The Lively Ghosts of Ireland

The Lively Ghosts of Ireland

HANS HOLZER

Illustrations by Catherine Buxhoeveden

DORSET PRESS
NEW YORK

This editon published by Dorset Press
by arrangement with Aspera Ad Astra, Inc.

ISBN 0-7607-2733-3 *paperback*

Printed and bound in the United States of America

01 02 03 04 MP 9 8 7 6 5 4 3 2 1

BVG

Illustrations

Contents

Contents

The Lively Ghosts of Ireland

You Don't Have to Be Irish to Like Ireland

THE FIRST TIME I SET FOOT ON IRISH SOIL WAS IN 1950 WHEN my New York-bound plane had to await better weather conditions at Shannon. It was evening, and the only Irishman I met on that occasion was TV emcee Ed Sullivan, returning home from one of his talent-buying expeditions.

But I became restless that summer night, and decided to take a walk all by myself down the road that leads to Limerick City. I did not see a leprechaun that moonlit August night, but I can't be at all sure that any did not see *me*.

Leprechauns have a curious way of pulling strings, I am told, and if the Little People put it into their heads to have me come to Ireland, as surely as there is a heaven, they would find a way!

My next brush with things Irish was at Murray Bernstein's house on West 16th Street, and if that doesn't sound too Irish, dear reader, don't be incredulous. For Mr. and Mrs. Bernstein had then just discovered what later became known as the *Search for Bridey Murphy,* and I was present when the first few tapes of their work were played for a handful of interested friends.

As the years went by, the big airplanes did not have to stop at Shannon any longer for refuelling purposes, which was a shame, since a lot of refuelling was also done by the passengers en route.

This worked a particular hardship on the people selling Irish whiskey and other potions at the duty-free airport shop, and, even sadder to report, the slack was later taken up by the London airport shop, which is really adding insult to injury.

As my interest in the occult grew and my library kept pace with it, I acquired James Reynolds' memorable two books on Irish ghosts, *Ghosts in Irish Houses* and *More Ghosts in Irish Houses*. Reynolds was as fine a water color artist as he was a poet and his illustrations are collector's items today. I had always wondered how much of his narrative was fact and what part was fiction, if any, and I was to find the true relationship between the two some years later on a lonely mountain road in the backwoods of Southern Ireland.

To my amazement I discovered that very little tangible had been written about Irish ghosts, except for Reynolds' books and the books of Sir Shane Leslie and Elliott O'Donnell, none of which exactly dealt with contemporary hauntings. But then I found out also that there wasn't even a really comprehensive tourist guide to all Ireland, the way one exists for practically every other country. In a way I was glad, for surely I could do without the usual tourist crowds to cramp my ghost-hunting style.

I had planned on going to Ireland for many years, but somehow I got sidetracked to England and the Continent. Then finally, my agent, Mrs. Cole, determinedly said, Why don't you write a book about Irish ghosts? Why didn't I indeed? *You don't have to be Irish to like Irish ghosts.*

Ireland was virgin territory to me as far as psychic experiences were concerned. I had received a handful of letters from people who had heard of my work, but I really needed help. I had learned the hard way that popular conceptions are often false. Everybody tells me—everybody, that is, who has not read my books, *Ghosts I've Met* and *Ghost Hunter* and *Yankee Ghosts*, and there are still some who haven't—that England is full of ghosts and practically every manor house just crawls with them. It was my destiny to find things a lot different.

The British home owner is frequently reluctant to talk about his ghosts, and there are more haunted houses in America than in Britain.

By the same token, I had been told that the Irish are just naturally prone to the supernatural, from leprechauns to ghosts, and I would have a field day the moment I set foot on the Ould Sod.

I did not want to take the chance of missing Ireland's ghosts, so I wrote to the Irish Tourist Board, the Bord Failte Eireann, as they say in Dublin, and the door opened rapidly after that. Ireland is a small country and its people are not ashamed to do things in a smallish way if that seems the best way to them.

Gordon Clark wrote to me in longhand, enclosing a magazine which had published an account of a haunting that might interest me. Because of this piece, I travelled some hundred and twenty miles over back roads to visit a haunted castle on the Kerry Coast.

"It seems astonishing that Ireland should be without at least one ghost," Mr. Clark wrote, "and if you decide to come, we will do whatever possible."

To this friendly hand was added later the helping arm of Paddy Byrnes, of the *Evening Herald* in Dublin, who had been running a long series of articles on ghosts in his paper.

When I got to Dublin, Byrnes kindly showed me the manuscript of his planned cyclopedia of ghostlore, and I made notes on a few of them that seemed to me capable of verification. For here lies the trouble not only with Irish ghost stories but with ghost stories in general—you can find lots of them, but precious few that stand up to a rigorous reporter's approach. If I can't find a witness or two to corroborate the experiences, they do not warrant further investigation from my point of view. After all, I am a parapsychologist and not merely a collector of tall tales.

I also called on the Irish Tourist office in New York on the off-chance that they might have something useful to me in their files. From the very first, I met the stiffest opposition. Ghosts? We don't have any. I mean, we don't know of any.

When you go on a safari to Africa, you prepare yourself properly and carry the tools of your trade. All I could do to prepare myself was study the map of Ireland, go over Reynolds' most likely sounding stories again, and pick the best prospects for a ghost hunt.

I had also appealed to the British psychic research people, on the theory that Ireland was, at the very least, a stepchild. The British College of Psychic Science, to which I also belong, had no knowledge of any research activities in Ireland, and the editor of the spiritualist newspaper in England was even more succinct in his appraisal of the situation: "Ireland is a priest-ridden country, and you won't find any psychic researchers there."

It is true, I did not find any students of the psychic in Ireland. Neither did I see any abundance of priests. So perhaps my editor friend was counting the dead ones, too. You never know with those spiritualists.

Having been warned of rainy seasons, of which Ireland allegedly has several, we decided to go in August, right after the Dublin horseshow, for surely no ghost hunter in his right mind would want to compete with the horseshow for the attention of the Irish.

It was suitably broiling in New York, and I was counting the days when we would descend upon the Emerald Isle. I had decided to work our way westward, and to start in the most remote part of Ireland first, then gradually travel towards the east and wind up in Dublintown. With spirits high, and clues low, we left for the airport, as New York sank slowly in its own steam behind us.

We arrived at Shannon airport on a bright and early morning, and the breakfast at the airport restaurant immediately drove home the fact we were on Irish soil. For the Irish oatmeal we then tasted for the first time has been a favorite of ours ever since. The service was remarkably fast and good and we were beginning to take that song about "a little bit of heaven" named Ireland seriously.

We had of course no intention of staying at the Shannon airport restaurant overnight. To the contrary, a very detailed plan of attack had been worked out by me to do as much ghost hunting in the limited time we had as possible. Originally, we had planned on staying at one of the hotels in the area, but Sybil Leek, our British psychic friend, had brought word that a lady decorator with whom she was friendly had just acquired a castle in the area and we would be most welcome to make our head-quarters there.

Now if there is one thing I like making my headquarters in, it is a castle. In the first place, the appointments are likely to be luxurious, the servants plentiful and the atmosphere larded with romance and excitement. Quite possibly, one might find a castle ghost in the bargain as well, for you know how it was with those old nobles—they did an awful lot of killing and many a castle contains not only a few skeletons in the family closet but some meandering spectres as well. Thus it was with high hopes and visions of medieval splendor that we set out for Kilcolgan Castle.

We had rented a local taxi, having shrewdly bargained for a flat rate beforehand. It would take us about two hours to wind ourselves north from the river Shannon area into County Galway, where said castle stood right at the seashore on the approaches to Galway City.

The ride was reasonably smooth, as we flitted past Limerick and Ennis and followed the coastal road towards Galway. Suddenly, the driver turned into a side road, far less smooth than what we had been travelling on, and the car came to an abrupt halt in front of what looked to me like a small tourist lodge built in the style of a watchtower. To the left of it there was a small guest house ready to take on the tired traveller.

Since it was only noon, we had no need for such an abode and at first it occurred to me that our driver had made a mistake. There would *have* to be another, more imposing *castle*.

He shook his head; no, this was it. We crawled out of the car, leaving our luggage behind for the moment. The gate to the garden was open and there was not a soul around. Had we accidentally found a ghost castle? As we wandered through the downstairs rooms, which reminded me of a Georgian backwoods sharecropper's hut, we began to wonder whether our hostess had not forgotten about our coming. Later it developed that she had merely forgotten the date. As we passed the unique bathroom and had a look at what must have been the most ancient part of the house, we realized at once that this was one castle where we could not possibly spend the night.

Sybil had told us of the view from this "castle," and a view there was indeed, over the mudflats stretching from the road towards the bay in the distance. I thought what a wonderful home this would make for a New Jersey mosquito to breed in, but it was not for us, and we were glad that we did not have to tell our no doubt well-meaning hostess that there are castles, and then, well, there are houses sold to American tourists as castles, if that is what they want to be sold.

We left Sybil behind us to brave at least one night as a matter of courtesy to her decorator friend, and then drove off to Galway City in quest of a hotel. Little did we realize that this was the height of the season and that everything was full up. Galway City struck me as a typical holiday resort overrun by tourists, mainly the local kind or from England, and we could not find suitable rooms there for love or money. By now it was afternoon and the matter became pressing. After a brief council of war, it was decided to return to the "castle" and see if it could be put in shape for a night at least. As we rounded the curve and saw it lying there, we were at once warmly greeted by Sybil, who had somehow felt we would return and take her away from all this. Courtesy be damned, she felt, and where could one find decent facilities and a bath?

Our driver, who was the quiet, country type, had observed all this without making any suggestions. But now he spoke up.

"I know just the place for you," he said and I wondered why he had not thought of it earlier. By now the fare was monumental. At a roadside telephone he called Dromoland Castle, and I rented two rooms there, sight unseen.

Perhaps this was a real castle. It was. It was magnificent and exactly what an American tourist of means would expect in an Irish castle. This was no coincidence. An enterprising American had bought the old O'Brien stronghold and fixed it up with modern appointments, as they say, including a U.S. flag on the roof and U.S. prices. But we were so glad to find elegance and proper service that we could not very well quarrel with this.

Everywhere we went in the large castle, which looked like a cross between Windsor Castle and Oxford University, there were life-sized pictures of members of the O'Brien family who had built the house originally in the 18th and 19th centuries. The O'Brien chieftains had been among those who had helped the survivors of the Spanish Armada come safely ashore in Western Ireland. Many Spaniards were not so welcomed, for 300 were hanged in one day alone in nearby Galway City by the English commander. But the O'Brien was still independent in 1588 and he helped those stricken sailors.

We spent three days at Dromoland, and enjoyed its beautiful, lush park to the utmost. There was a flower garden, too, built along cloister lines, and an overall peace and elegance that made this a really restful place. The waitresses, charming country girls all, wore red and white outfits, the O'Brien colors, and candles adorned each and every table in the dining room.

It was not surprising that this castle had a regal feeling about it, for the O'Briens of Western Ireland, who owned many houses here, were descended directly from Ireland's famed Highking Brian Boru, who ruled across country at Tara in the early 11th century.

Because Ireland, especially the West country, is very moist, the vegetation here is almost too rich and one sometimes has the feeling of walking in a jungle of ferns and century-old trees. Walking down a long and dark lane, towards a white marble gazebo looming up in the distance, my wife Catherine and I found our feet sinking into the wet soil. There is an awful lot of bog—local term for swamp—in this part of Ireland, and stories of ghosts of men killed in the bog are numerous. It was a favorite form of killing one's enemy—drive him into the bog, and the swamp will do the rest.

We were now in County Clare, only eight miles from Shannon airport, as we discovered when we paid our driver his fare. It had been an expensive tour just to view a non-castle and to wind up in a genuine castle we had never heard of before.

Soon I discovered that even so recent an addition to Ireland's stately houses can have a family spectre.

Some years ago, novelist Annie Smithson was staying at the castle. She was not looking for ghosts; in fact, she could not have cared less had she met one.

It so happened that she did, however. Suddenly looking up, she found herself face to face with a woman who had come out of thin air. Before she could challenge the stranger, the woman vanished. A moment before, Miss Smithson had been quite alone in the room.

I asked Sybil Leek if she felt a presence at Dromoland. Either the lady ghost is too shy to spook for American tourists, or the changes in decor effected when Dromoland became a country club were too confusing for her. At any rate, Sybil felt nothing, and there haven't been any reports of the ghost in recent years either.

We spent the next morning poring over maps, and then drove off with a local driver in search of haunted houses. Dromoland's chef thoughtfully provided us with a basket lunch, in case we would find ourselves miles from nowhere when the call of the stomach came. The Irish like to eat, and even though ghosts don't, ghost hunters should.

The Case of the I.R.A. Ghosts

IT WAS A SUNNY, PLEASANTLY COMFORTABLE DAY WHEN THE first expedition on Irish soil started out from the elegant confines of Dromoland Castle. Soon we left behind the international feeling of the main highway, and made our way towards the southern shore of the river Shannon which at this point is as wide as a lake.

We left behind us the bleak masonry of Limerick City, with its factories and wharves, and people going off to work. For it was a weekday and the non-tourist population of Ireland had other things to do than loaf around.

At Tarbert, we left the winding shore road and struck out inland, directly south for Listowel. We arrived in this sleepy old town around noon, just in time to have lunch at the local inn, its only hotel of some size, set back to the side of the old square still covered by cobblestones as in centuries gone by.

It was quite a sight we gave the townspeople, Catherine, elegant as ever, Sybil Leek in purple, and me, heavily burdened with tape recorders and cameras. It is to the eternal credit of the people of Listowel that no one ever asked us any questions, or perhaps this is part of the Irish spirit—to accept people as

9

they are. At any rate, we had a pleasant meal and I went to the telephone to see what I could do about some local help.

Now the telephone is something of a rarity in Western Ireland. I mean one that works.

Our first encounter with this intrusion of the 20th century into Irish life came at Kilcolgan Castle, that non-castle we never got to sleep in. There was a phone there which I at first took for a toy. It was light and the cord seemed to lead nowhere, but little did I know that this was it—the phone. It actually works at times, except that several hours each day it is off. The trouble is, they never tell you when. Consequently it is best to have emergencies only after you've checked the phone.

Here in Listowel I also discovered that you needed certain coins to operate the telephone properly. So I went into the bar to get some change, for to carry a large supply of pennies around was not my idea of light travelling.

The traditional Irish friendliness was quite evident here, and more so in the bar. There were only two guests having a drink at the counter, one of them an Irish priest originally from San Francisco, who had decided to return to Listowel and really *live*. I had been given the name of a playwright named Eamon Keane who might be in a position to help me find Mr. Maloney's haunted houses. I had heard about these haunted houses from Mr. Maloney himself in New York.

*　　*　　*

I was doing a radio program in New York in May of 1965 on which I suggested that any Irishman with an authentic experience involving ghosts should contact me.

One of those who rose to the occasion was Patrick Maloney of Queens Village, about an hour from my home. Mr. Maloney had lived in New York for forty-three years, but had originally come from Listowel, Ireland. Mr. Maloney is a man in his early sixties, full of good cheer and about as factual as any man in his position would be. For Mr. Maloney is the supervisor of hospital aides in one of the larger mental institutions near New York. His work demands a great deal of common sense, dealing, as he does, with those who have lost theirs. As if his relationship with things medical were not enough to give Mr. Maloney a sense of caution, he is also an accomplished amateur magician and a student of hypnosis. He knows all about the tricks of the mind and the tricks of clever prestidigitators. He has met such famous magic craftsmen as Dunninger and Harry Blackstone, and to this day attends weekly meetings of the magicians' circle in New York, to keep up on the latest tricks and to sharpen his sense of illusion.

Now if there is one group of diehard skeptics, it is the magicians. To most magicians, all psychic manifestations must be fraudulent because they can make some of them. But the inability of most sleight-of-hand artists to accept the reality of extrasensory perception is based on a philosophical concept. To them, all is material, and if there are illusions they did not create, then their whole world is no longer secure.

To his eternal credit, Patrick Maloney is an exception to this breed. That this is so is due largely to his own psychic experiences. He is a Roman Catholic in good standing, married, and a grandfather many times over. One of his married daughters also has had psychic experiences, proving again that the talent does sometimes get handed down in a family, usually on the female side.

"I always keep an open mind; that's the way we learn," he commented in his note to me.

Born in Ireland in 1901, he went to National School and finished the 8th grade. Later he lived in England for a few years prior to settling in America. It was during his youth in Ireland that he became aware of his psychic gifts.

I met Patrick Maloney and we went over his experiences in great detail.

"It was the year 1908 when I had my first memorable experience," he began, "and I was about seven years old at the time. We were living in the town of Listowel, County Kerry, in an old house on Convent Street. The house is still standing; it is built of limestone and has a slate roof.

"That day I was home, taking care of one of my younger brothers who was still a baby in a crib. My mother had gone down to the store, so while she was out, I went upstairs to look at some picture books which were kept on the first landing of the stairs. Upstairs there were two empty rooms, one facing the other, and they were not used by us.

"I was going over the picture books, when something made me look up.

"There, on the second landing, was a little man no more than five feet tall, beckoning me with his right hand to come to him!

"I can see him as clearly today as if it had just happened. He wore black clothes and his skin was dark, the color of copper, and on his head he had a skull cap with brass bells, and all the time he was laughing and motioning me to come up."

"Weren't you scared?" I interjected. What a strange sight this must have been in the sleepy little town of Listowel.

Mr. Maloney shook his head.

"Not at all," he said. "Maybe I was too young to be afraid properly, but I knew as young as I was that this was a strange thing, so I put my books down and went back downstairs. I had seen the little man come from a totally empty room and walk into another equally empty room, and I knew there was something queer about all this. But I never told my mother about it until I was a grown man."

"Did your mother offer any explanation?"

"No, she didn't. She just listened quietly and never said a word. To this day I have no idea who the little man was."

I wondered about it myself and made a mental note to have a look at the house on Convent Street, Listowel.

But the encounter with the Unknown that puzzled him most happened in 1918 when Patrick Maloney was 17 years of age. At that time there was a great deal of what the Irish euphemistically call "the trouble"—guerrilla warfare between the British occupation forces and the outlawed I.R.A., the Irish Republican Army. This group of citizen-soldiers contributed considerably to Irish independence later, and there is scarcely a spot in all Ireland where there isn't a grave or two of these "freedom fighters." Unfortunately, when the Irish Republic came into being and normal relations returned between the English and their erstwhile enemies, the I.R.A. decided to continue the struggle.

Principally, the six northern counties known as Ulster are the bone of contention. The Irish government in Dublin would like to have solved the problem peacefully and gradually, but the I.R.A. could not wait, so there was violence once again, frequently to the detriment of famed landmarks, until eventually the I.R.A. was outlawed by its own government.

The "Black and Tans" of 1918 engaged in battles and skirmishes all over the land. Nobody could be sure that a stray bullet would not hit an innocent bystander. About two miles outside the town of Listowel, there was a gate in the side of the road. Behind it, the British were waiting. An I.R.A. patrol, consisting of three men, was approaching the spot. In the ensuing ambush, two of the Irish irregulars were killed by the British. Years later, a large Celtic cross was erected over the graves, but the story itself, being similar to so many tragedies of like nature all over Ireland, became dimmed, and even the local people scarcely remember the spot.

That moonlit night in 1918, however, a young Paddy Maloney and a friend, Moss Barney, of Ballybunnon, Kerry, were bicycling down that road, eager to get to Listowel for the night. They had been to a place called Abbyfeale, about five miles away, to see a circus. It was the month of June, and around 1:00 in the morning, with the moon illuminating the road rather well. At that time, the monument did not exist, of course, and the shooting was still within memory. But the two travellers gave it no thought. It did not concern them; they were in a gay mood after a pleasant evening at the circus.

When they reached the spot in the road where the ambush

had happened, something stopped them in their tracks. No matter how hard Patrick tried to ride on, he could not move from the spot.

"It felt as if someone were in back of us, holding on to our bicycles. I felt clammy and moist, and the sense of a presence behind me trying to prevent me from going down that road was very strong. I had the sensation that someone was trying to keep us *from running into trouble* farther down the road.

"I tried to bicycle as hard as I could, but to no avail. Yet, the road was level, with a stretch of wooded section for at least 500 feet. I felt myself weaken, and the cold sweat broke out all over me. I tried to tell Moss about my difficulties but found my tongue was paralyzed.

"With a last surge of power, I pushed on and finally broke away from the 'thing' behind me. As soon as we came out of the wooded section our bikes were free as before. We both jumped off and I started to tell Moss what I had experienced—only to find that he, too, had felt the same uncanny weight. He, too, was unable to talk for a while.

"'I'll never ride this road again at night,' he finally said, and meant it."

"Did you have other psychic experiences after that?" I asked, for it was plain to me that Patrick Maloney was mediumistic to a degree, having experienced such physical manifestations.

"Many times," he acknowledged.

"When I worked as a psychiatric aide in one of the hospitals here," Maloney added, "I had a most unusual experience. It was late at night and I was very tired. I went into a linen room there, and I lay down on a table to rest a bit, afraid I might fall asleep during the night when I was on duty. I was only down about five minutes, with a blanket underneath me, when someone came along and pulled that blanket from under me. Now I weigh over two hundred pounds, and yet it all happened so fast I had that blanket on top of me before I knew it."

"Was there anyone else in the room?" I inquired.

"Nobody in the room, nobody in the ward, just myself."

"What did you do?"

"I jumped up and looked around. The patients were all sleeping. So I went back to rest. Then it happened again, only this time it felt like a big, heavy hand feeling my back. That did it. I came out and locked the room up."

"What did you make of it?" I said.

"When I went to investigate the ward, I found a patient dead. He had died in his sleep. He was an ex-boxer. He had been under my personal care."

"I guess he wanted to let you know he was going on," I said. "Any other uncanny experiences?"

"Oh yes," Maloney said matter-of-fact like, "my son died in 1945, and a couple of months after he died, I was sitting in my home watching television. I was comfortable, with my legs stretched out, when I felt a person cross by my legs very fast. It made a swishing sound. I looked at my wife, but she had not moved at all. I knew it was my son, for he had a peculiar walk."

Maloney has had numerous true dreams, and often knows when a person is "not long for this world." Like the co-worker at the hospital whom he had dubbed the "dead man." For two years he did not realize why he felt that way about his colleague. Then the man committed suicide.

In 1946 he returned to Ireland again after a long absence. Suddenly, in his hotel room, he heard his wife Catherine's voice clear across from America. That week, her mother died.

Maloney takes his gift casually. He neither denies it nor does he brag about it. He is very Irish about it all.

* * *

When the priest from San Francisco heard I was trying to phone Eamon Keane for an appointment, he laughed.

"Nonsense," he intoned, "just go to his house and introduce yourself. We're all very friendly here."

Mr. Keane, it turned out, also had an unlisted number. Imagine, an unlisted number in *Listowel!* But playwrights will have ideas.

Lunch being done with, we proceeded to find Mr. Keane. I had also been informed that in addition to playwriting, he owned a bar. We walked up the road and found ourselves in front of a bar marked "Keane's." Had we come to the right place? We had not.

"You want my brother," the owner said, and off we went again, a block farther up the road, to another bar, also marked "Keane's." In fact, I don't recall much else on that street except bars—here called pubs.

Mr. Keane was most helpful. He knew what I was looking for, and he offered to take me to a man who had had some experiences and could tell me about them firsthand. So we left again and drove down a few blocks to a small house the ground floor of which was occupied by a store. The owner of the store, it developed, was the man to see. He dealt in fishing tackle.

John Garen had lived here for fifty-seven years and he had an accent to prove it.

I asked if he knew of any ghosts.

"Right here in this street, sir," he replied, "there is a house with a little brook beside it, and there was a family by the name of Loughneanes living in it. It's on Convent Street and called Glauna Foka."

"What does that mean?" I asked, my Gaelic being extremely weak.

"Glen of the Fairies," Mr. Garen replied. "I've never seen any, but it seems that chairs and everything that was inside the house would be thrown out the windows, and you'd hear the glass crashing, and when you'd come around there'd be nobody there. The people had to move out because of it. This was about sixty years ago."

I thanked Mr. Garen for his information, such as it was, and wished him the top of the afternoon. Then we drove on and stopped in front of the house on Convent Street where Patrick Maloney had seen the little fellow with the fool's cap.

The house had obviously been reconditioned and did not show its age at all. It was a two-story affair, with a garden in back, and

Sybil Leek went across the street to have a quiet look at it. We could not get in, for the present owners were not too keen on the subject of ghosts. Mr. Garen asked us not to mention his name, in particular, for in a town the size of Listowel, *everything* gets around eventually.

"What do you sense here?" I asked Sybil, who of course knew nothing whatever of Patrick Maloney, his experiences, or even Mr. Garen's recent talk.

"There undoubtedly have been some manifestations in the upper right-hand room," Sybil said succinctly, "and I think this has an association with water. I think the previous owner was in some occupation in which water was very important. Someone associated with a mill, I think."

Sybil did not know that there was a brook beside the house, nor that there had once been a mill not far away.

"How long ago do you think this happened?"

"About two hundred years ago," she replied. "On the side of the house where there is no building at the moment, I can see, in my mind's eye, a smaller building, rather flat."

"How far back do you feel manifestations took place here?"

"About four years ago, then around 1948, and before that, about a hundred and twenty years ago. There has been some tragedy connected with water. I sense some wheels around that mill, and a name that sounds like Troon to me."

We drove on, out of Listowel now, towards where the mill once stood.

"On the right side," Sybil murmured, and Mr. Keane confirmed the location.

Since we could not get into the house itself I decided it was best to look into still another house Patrick Maloney had told me about. Mr. Keane excused himself and hurried back to his bar. We drove on into the open countryside looking for a farm house of which we knew little, if anything.

Mr. Maloney had provided me with a rough, hand-drawn map and it came in handy.

"The house in Greenville Road," he had explained, "near the

mill, had some poltergeist activity when I was there. The kitchen is haunted, and the bedroom also. Clothes used to be pulled off people in bed and the room used to fill up with roaches—millions of them—and then they would vanish into thin air; faces were seen at the windows, looking in. Fights were taking place, tables pushed around and chairs also, and the cups and saucers would dance on their shelves in the closet. The Connors who lived there are all dead now, and others live there, but I don't know them. This was about forty-five years ago."

All this came to mind again as we rode down the bumpy road looking for the old Connors house.

A smallish, one-story farm house was pointed out to us by an elderly man working beside the road. It turned out to be a Connors house all right, but the wrong Connors. Our Connors were farther down the road, and finally we found the house that fit Maloney's description and map.

Someone had evidently just moved in recently and was in the process of fixing it up. This activity had not yet extended to the garden around the house, which was lovely in its wild ways, totally untouched by human hands for years, evidently.

There was a broad iron gate closing off the garden from the road. The sun was not so high any more and the picture was one of utmost peace and tranquillity. Carefully—for there are more dogs in Ireland than anywhere else in the world—carefully I opened the gate and walked towards the house. My feet sank into the wet ground but I carried on. At the door I was greeted by a young woman in her late twenties who bid us welcome in the typical Irish country way of welcoming a stranger. Catherine and Sybil came along a moment later, and we had a look at what was once the haunted house of the Connors.

"Mrs. Healy," I began, "you moved in here a few days ago. This used to be the Connors house—am I right?"

"That is correct," she replied in almost brogue-free speech. "It is a pretty old house, but it has been reconditioned recently."

The house was a happy one to her; at any rate neither she nor her husband nor their small child had noticed anything unusual —yet.

Sybil stepped inside the house now. It was really nothing more than a smallish kitchen, a hall, and a bedroom, all on the same floor. Immediately she felt in another era.

"When the woman was talking to you just now," Sybil said, "I heard another voice. A man's voice. It's a strong voice, but I can't understand it."

"Is it Gaelic?" I asked.

"I should think so. It's the inflection of the voice that is peculiar to me. It is a hard, strong voice. There is water connected with this place."

"Any tragedy?"

"The man is connected with it. Turn of the century. He had some trouble with his head, probably due to a blow. The injury affected his life very drastically. Ultimately led to his death, but was not immediately responsible for it. A very angry person, I'd say."

We did not want to overstay our welcome at the farm house, so I thanked Mrs. Healy for letting us visit.

"There is just one more thing," she said pensively. "You see this gate over there?" We nodded, for I had admired it from the start.

"Well," Mrs. Healy said somewhat sheepishly, "no matter how often I close it, it just does not want to stay closed."

*   *   *

The afternoon was growing slowly old, and we still had two other places to visit. We drove back through Listowel and out the other end, following Patrick Maloney's crudely drawn map. Nobody in Listowel could direct us towards the monument at the crossroads we were seeking, and we wasted an hour going up and down wrong country roads. It is not easy to get directions in the Irish countryside, for few people know more than their immediate neighborhood. Finally we hit paydirt. Ahead of us there was a crossroad that seemed to fit Maloney's description, with the wooded area on one side. But no Celtic cross in sight!

I was puzzled. Leaving Sybil with Catherine in the car, I set out on foot to explore the land beyond the road. About twenty yards inside the area, I suddenly came upon the monument. Our driver, whose name was Sylvester, also was puzzled. He had never heard of such a monument in this place. But there it was, set back from prying eyes, a gray-white stone wall, about two feet high, beyond which stood a tall Celtic cross. Before the cross were three graves, inscribed only in Gaelic. Beyond the graves the hill sloped gently towards the faraway Kerry Coast.

The weather had become rainy and dark clouds were hanging overhead.

I asked Sybil to come forward now, and before she had a chance to look at the marble plaques on the ground, I asked for her impressions at this shrine.

"There is peace here, but only on the outside. On my right there seems to be an old building in the distance. I feel it is connected with this spot. It is a tragic, desperate spot, with a lot of unhappiness, helplessness—something had to happen here. There is mental torture."

"Did anyone die here?" I said. Sybil stepped forward and looked at the graves.

"Yes," she replied immediately, "as you see yourself the inscriptions are in Gaelic and I don't understand Gaelic, but I think this was forty years ago, between forty and fifty years ago—there was fighting, and it was unexpected. Coming again from the right of me, some mortal conflict involving death of several people——"

"How many people?"

"I can see two," Sybil replied, and it occurred to me at once that she had no knowledge of the fact that *two* I.R.A. men had perished at this spot.

"Are there any presences here still?"

"The two, because these are the people that I feel. Why, I don't know, but again, the building on my right seems to interest the people and myself. Two men. Perhaps they're only guarding something. Something to watch in this area, always watching the countryside. Perhaps they had to watch the countryside *and still must do so!*"

"Quite," I said, thinking of the detail the patrol had been assigned—to watch the countryside.

Sybil closed her eyes for a moment.

"Why are they still here, so long after?" I inquired.

"Yes," she replied, "it is still of importance to them in this time and place, as it was then."

"But there is peace in the country now."

"I don't think there is peace in this particular part of the country," Sybil countered, and I knew, of course, that the I.R.A. is far from dead, especially in the rural areas.

"Do you get any names for these men?"

"No, but I can describe them to you. One is a broad-set man, and he has a rough face, country man, or forced to take to the country, not well kept, must have been hiding; he has a thick neck, and very brown eyes, perhaps five feet eight. There is someone with him, not related, but they've been together for some time. The building on the right has some connection with them."

There was a small house on the hill about a hundred yards farther back from the road.

"What outfits are these men in, Sybil?"

"I don't see uniforms," she replied, "very ordinary dress, trousers."

"Are they regular soldiers?"

"No—ordinary clothes of about forty-five years ago."

That would make it 1920—pretty close to the year 1918 in which Patrick Maloney had had his ghostly experience here.

"Are they serving any kind of outfit other than military?"

"Serving something, but I don't know what. No uniforms, but they are serving."

"How are they then serving, by what means?"

"Something noisy. I think they've been shot. One in the shoulder, near the heart."

"Can we help them in any way?"

"Somehow this place is . . . as if someone must always watch from here. This watching must go on. I don't know why they have to watch. They do."

"Are they aware of the present?"

"I don't think so. The one I described is more in evidence than the other. Perhaps he was leading. There is a need for silence here."

I then asked Sybil to inform the two men that the war was long over and they should return home to their families, that in fact, they were relieved of duty.

Sybil told them this, and that the crossroads were now safe. They had done their job well.

"Any reaction?" I asked after a moment.

"The main man still stands," Sybil reported, "but the other one is gone now."

Again, I asked Sybil to send the man away.

"Patrick is his name," Sybil said, and later I checked the name in the largest panel on the ground—Padraic it was.

A moment later, Sybil added: "I think he goes to the right now—what was to the right?"

"I don't know," I said truthfully.

Half a mile up the hill, the ruined house stood silently.

"That's where they had to go back to. He is gone now. There is nothing."

And so it is that the two ghostly I.R.A. men finally went home on extended leave.

BALLYHEIGUE, KERRY
IRELAND

C. Bushnell
6-66

Ballyheigue Is Calling, or
The Ghost on the Kerry Coast

I F YOU'VE NEVER HEARD OF BALLYHEIGUE—PRONOUNCED JUST like Rodgers' and Hammerstein's Bali-ha'i—you've really missed one of the most poetic stretches of coastland still unspoiled by human greed. It isn't completely untouched by habitation by any means, but there isn't—as yet—that glass-and-concrete luxury hotel, the nearby airport, the chic clientele. Ballyheigue just sits there, a small fishing village and a majestic castle, looking out onto the Atlantic. This stretch of land used to swarm with smugglers not so long ago, as it was rather difficult for the revenue people to catch up with the wily Irish in the many bays and loughs of Western Ireland.

Now I wasn't looking for smugglers' coves or new sources of poteen, but the spirit that moved me to travel down the Kerry coast had been brought to my attention in a respectable magazine piece, published a couple of years ago in Dublin. The article, entitled "On the Trail of a Ghost," is the factual report of Captain P. D. O'Donnell, about his strange experiences at Ballyheigue in 1962. The magazine, *Ireland of the Welcomes*, is published by the Irish Tourist Board, but this piece is the only instance of a psychic adventure appearing in its pages. Here then is Captain O'Donnell's report:

"It all started during a normal vacation in Ballyheigue in the first, sunny half of June, 1962. Even on holidays, a part-time writer like myself is always on the lookout for new ideas, but on that vacation I was determined to get the most out of a heat wave, and to heck with writing. I relaxed in the quiet atmosphere of the almost deserted village, lazed on the lonely four-mile-long beach with the family, or joined in the beach games with the handful of visitors from the hotel.

"Then, one day—it was the 4th or 5th day of June, be it noted—I took a walk with my eight-year-old son, Frank, up the winding avenue above the cliffs to the burnt-out shell of Ballyheigue Castle. It was purely in deference to my interest in old castles, and to show my son the castle. I had only a vague idea of its history, but knew that from here the strong Crosbie family had once lorded it over most of the north of County Kerry. They left the country when the republicans burnt the castle to the ground during the 'troubles' of 1921.

"For a while we talked to an old man working nearby, and he told us the castle was never explored fully. Then with camera in hand we started. I am one for always trying different angles and unusual shots with a camera, so when our short tour among the ruins satisfied Frank, we started to take a few snaps for the record. The snap that mattered was taken inside the castle. Frank was placed standing against a wall at right angles to the front of the castle, and I stood back. It was shadowy inside the castle, but the sun was slanting strongly through a window on his right. In the viewfinder I was able to get Frank on the left and hoped also to get the view of the beach through the window on the right. The light of the sun coming through the window would be enough, I hoped—no light meters for my amateur photography.

"The story of the rest of the vacation does not matter, except to record that the days were filled with sunshine, battling the breakers, looking for Kerry diamonds on Kerry Head, enjoying the relaxation and joining in the hotel sing-song at night. What did matter, however, was when the color film came back from the developers. The snap which I have described appeared to have another figure in it, partly obscured by the square of light that was the window. This figure held a sword, and its legs were not trousered, but appeared as if clothed in hose or thigh boots! At first I thought this rather frightening, but my wife passed it off as a double exposure.

"However, when she and I examined the other snapshots, we both agreed that there was neither a double exposure nor any other negative which if it was superimposed on the 'ghost' picture could have produced the same effect. What then was the answer, we wondered. Was it really a ghost I had photographed?

"The events that followed, indeed, made the affair more extraordinary. I brought the snap into the office, and passed it around my friends. Two were more interested than the others, and asked to see the negative. When I went home for lunch I slipped the negative into the same envelope with the snapshot —much to my later regret—and they were suitably impressed. That night, however, I gave the envelope to a friend, forgetting that the negative was also inside—and would you believe it— the envelope disappeared most mysteriously. If it was only the snapshot, it would have been all right, but as the negative was with it, all was lost. At least I had twelve witnesses who saw both negative and print, so anyone who says I am a liar can call them liars too.

"Of course, I advertised in the newspapers, and even got leaflets printed offering a very good reward, but my 'ghost' picture never turned up. I was interviewed by a newspaper and on radio, and determined to look into the whole matter of recent Irish ghostly appearances and write a book on the subject. The news travelled, and shortly after, I had queries from Stockholm and from Copenhagen seeking to buy the Swedish and Danish rights of the photographs. They were offering sums from £25 to £30, and if I had the photo, I would probably have been the richer by much more, when other newspapers got interested.

"Why were the Danes so interested in a photograph of a 'ghost' from the wilds of Kerry? That story is extremely interesting. According to old Kerry records a Danish ship, the *Golden Lyon*, of the Danish Asiatic Company, en route from Copenhagen to Tranquebar, was wrecked on the strand at Ballyheigue on October 20, 1730. It had been blown off its course by a fierce storm, but the local story was that the Crosbies of Ballyheigue Castle set up false lights on horses' heads to lure the ship ashore. The ship's captain, thinking the bobbing lights ahead from other shipping, kept on course, only to become a wreck on the Atlantic breakers.

"The crew were rescued by Sir Thomas Crosbie and his tenants. Also salvaged were many bottles of Danish wine, clothing, equipment, *and* twelve chests of silver bars and coin. The last was for the purpose of paying for goods and labor in Tranquebar, and was the cause of six people meeting their deaths. Soon afterwards, Sir Thomas Crosbie died suddenly, by poison it was rumored, and his wife, Lady Margaret, claimed a sum of £4,500 for salvage and the loss of her husband. She said it was because of his labors and exertions on the night of the wreck that he died. The ship's master, Captain J. Heitman, opposed the claim indignantly, and moved the twelve chests of silver down into the cellar under the strong tower of the castle. However, delay followed delay, and by June, 1731, he still found he could not get the silver safely to Dublin, and home to Denmark, or on another ship.

"Then one night he was aroused by the sound of many voices outside the castle gates. Jumping up, he was left under no illusions that a raid was in progress. About fifty or sixty men with blackened faces stormed the gates, and attacked the tower. Lady Margaret then arrived and flung herself in front of the captain, saying he would be killed if he ventured outside. Meanwhile, the sentry on the door to the cellar rushed, bleeding from stab wounds, up to his comrades on the first floor of the tower. He told them that his two fellow sentries lay dead outside, and that the mob had disarmed him. As the other Danes had only one musket between them and little ammunition—another bone of contention between Heitman and Lady Margaret—they retreated to the top room of the tower and were spectators to the scene of the twelve chests of silver being loaded on farm carts. Then the shouting stopped and the carts vanished into the night.

"However, within three days, Sir Edward Denny, the governor of Tralee, had nine men in Tralee gaol. One of the Danes had spotted a nephew of Lady Margaret's in the mob, and it soon became apparent that the whole robbery was planned by friends of the Crosbies. In the dispositions taken before the several trials, a number of the accused stated that four chests of the silver had been laid aside for Lady Margaret. These were never recovered. Lady Margaret denied knowing anything about the affair, and the Danes recovered only £5,000 out of a total of £20,000 in silver. Some of the raiders fled across the Shannon to Clare, others left for France in a fishing boat loaded with silver, while the majority simply went to earth and said nothing.

"Two Crosbies, relatives of Lady Margaret, were tried in Dublin and acquitted, but a third man, named Cantillon, a tenant of the castle Crosbies, was found guilty. One man hanged himself in Tralee gaol and another, who turned state's evidence, was found dead in his lodgings in Dublin. It was said he was poisoned, although the castle put it out that he died of typhoid and drinking too much. And the local tradition handed down the story that most of the gentry of north Kerry were involved. The castle at Ballyheigue was owned by the Cantillons, ancestors of the man found guilty, before the Crosbies arrived in Kerry. They were originally de Cantillons, who came to Ireland with the Norman invaders.

"Pieces of Danish china still exist locally, and in the cellars of Ballyheigue Castle lie some bottles with Danish crests, but of the missing silver there is still no trace. Some of the accused said it was buried in the orchard there, others that it was buried in an orchard three miles away near Banna Strand, and still others that it was buried behind Ballysheen House. If you enquire today in Ballyheigue, you will surely find someone who will tell you that he knows where it is buried, that he and his forefathers were afraid to dig it up, and maybe he might let you into the secret!

"The Danes are naturally still interested. It would make great copy if the 'ghost' photo was of one of the Danish sailors, and besides there is the lost treasure in silver. Long ago in the time of King Brian Boru, Viking ships of Norsemen and Danes raided Ireland, established the cities of Dublin, Wexford and Waterford, and brought loot back to Scandinavia. It was probably a simple matter for those envious of the Danish silver to persuade the local farmers that the presence of Danish silver in Ballyheigue Castle was a chance to reverse the flow of loot, and besides there was the landlord's wife, who lost her husband saving the shipwrecked Danes. However, the affair of the ghost picture has a more interesting history.

"All these historical details were new to me, and I found it highly interesting to read that swordsmen did indeed flash their swords in the castle. What was almost fantastic, however, was a little detail that almost escaped my notice. Remember, I said I had come on vacation to Ballyheigue in June. I arrived on June 1st. The second week was wild and rainy and it was not possible to take any color pictures in that week. The first week, however, was heat wave weather, with sunshine for 15 hours every day. It was after the week-end of 1st/2nd of June that I began to take the second roll of color film, and I am reasonably certain that the 'ghost' picture was taken on the 4th or 5th of June. Now, the record states that the Danish Silver Raid took place at midnight on June 4, 1731! Coincidence? Or do swords flash in Ballyheigue Castle on every June 4th when three Danish sailors died?

"You may bet I will be there next June 4th, with camera at the ready. Do I believe in this ghost? Well, it's a good excuse for visiting that charming spot again. Will I be afraid, while waiting there till midnight? Not on your life. I won't be alone, but somehow I don't believe we will see anything at night. The 'ghost' photo was taken in mid-afternoon with the sun slanting through the window from the west. Possibly, what I photographed was an imprint on the wall. But then again, the Danes were there, they were probably wearing seaboots, and there was swordplay there on the 4th of June."

*   *   *

So much for Captain O'Donnell's experience. The irony of losing his negative can be appreciated—for I too guard my psychic photographs, such as those of the ghostly monks at Winchester Cathedral, England, as if they were treasures, which in a way they are.

I made inquiries about the author of the article and was assured his integrity was the highest. As an officer he was not given to imagining things.

We had been visiting Listowel and decided to continue on to Ballyheigue. On the map it seemed an easy hour's ride, but it was almost sundown by the time we rounded the last hill and saw the sparkling sea before us.

Quickly passing through the village, we drove up to the gate of the castle. There was an old gatekeeper in a tiny house nearby and we had no trouble convincing her that we meant the castle no harm. We opened the old gate ourselves and then the car drove up the winding driveway towards the gray castle, the ruins of which loomed large over the landscape. The gentle slope reaching from its ramparts to the sandy shore were covered by meadowland, which was moist, as so much of Ireland is. On the land were perhaps two dozen cows and many more mementos of their presence.

We avoided the cows and parked the car close to the castle walls. Then I started to film the scene, while our driver ate a belated luncheon. The cows did not seem to bother him.

The castle looked eerie even in the daytime, with its windows staring out into the country like the eyes of a blind man. Inside, the walking was hazardous, for wet soil had long filled in the rooms. The fire that had devoured the castle in 1921 had left nothing of the interior standing, and the totally gutted heart of the once proud house now looked like an ancient Roman ruin. We walked about the many rooms, and Sybil tried to pick up impressions. Naturally, she knew nothing whatever about the place.

Ultimately, we followed her into one of the first-floor rooms looking out to the sea—a room whence one could have easily observed the ships and all that came and went. Here she stopped and listened, as if from within. Her psychic voice was giving her directions and we waited quietly for her words.

"Sybil, what do you think happened here?" I decided to break the silence.

"Whatever happened here," she replied hesitatingly, "certainly happened at a much lower level than the one we're on. I have a feeling that there is an underground passage connected with the sea."

She did not, of course, know about the Danish sailors and how the silver was hidden.

"I don't think I'm going back more than 150 years," she added, "although I know there are influences here going back three hundred years."

I urged her on, as she hesitated.

"This passage leading to the sea, Sybil—who came through it?" I asked.

"The name I have in mind is Donald," she replied. "I have a feeling of three young men, possibly sons, connected with the house, but Donald was not. The house was a large family house, but the people who came through the passage were travellers . . . *seafaring folk*."

Again I thought, how would Sybil know, consciously, of the Danish sailors coming here for refuge? She could not know this.

"Were they of local origin?" I asked.

"Foreign," she shot back, "probably coming from France. Lots of coming and going here."

"Why had these men come to the house?"

"Some connection with food," Sybil replied, not at all sure of her impression now, "food or something for the table."

"Any tragedy here?"

"Not those coming from France but the people living in the house."

"What happened?"

"There is the influence of a woman, the name is, I think, Emily, but the woman is connected with the house. The tragedy is through the woman. At first I had only the feeling of a man here, but now the woman is very strong."

"A man?"

"Men," Sybil corrected herself, and added: "The name Glen comes to me. The man's fate in the house . . . something to do with the food. Could it be poison? He was eating, when something happened."

One should realize at this point that Sybil had said several things that were pretty close to the true facts. Sir Thomas Crosbie, owner of the castle, was poisoned shortly after the Danish wreck had been salvaged. Was Lady Margaret as guilty of this sudden death as of the "raid" on the Danish silver staged later on?

Also, the raiders eventually fled to France by boat. Had Sybil felt this event somehow? But I wanted to hear more of what my psychic friend had to say here in the ruined drawing room of Ballyheigue Castle.

"I have a feeling of a man going down the passage. I think he was drowned because he disappears in the sea."

"Any fighting here?" I asked.

"I don't feel it now," Sybil said. "The woman is not constant to this house; she comes or goes away. The conflict is between the sea and the house. I think it could be a family feud. There is something else but I am not getting it as clearly as I am getting a foreign influence here."

"Other than French?"

"Also, there is a Northern influence. Many foreign visitors.

Beyond Scotland, Sweden. Fair men, Nordic influence. Two periods."

Sybil, of course, knew nothing about the Danish sailors.

Who was Emily? Who was Donald?

Did Captain O'Donnell indeed photograph the Danish silver raid, when the Danish sailors died defending their property in Ballyheigue castle?

Not having examined the photograph, I cannot attest to its genuineness, but I have taken similar pictures elsewhere and know it can be done. Thus I have no reason to doubt the story so movingly told by the Captain.

The silver may still lie somewhere underneath the crumbled walls of the castle. The Danes, as we know, only managed to get a fourth of their treasure out of there in the long run. And there may well be an 18th century swordsman defending it now as of yore.

It really does not matter. When you stand at the empty windows of Ballyheigue Castle and look out into the bay towards Kerry Head as the sun slowly settles behind the water line, you can well believe that the place is haunted.

As we rode back towards County Clare, it became chilly and the moisture in the air came down as light rain.

Nobody spoke much.

At one point, we almost took a wrong turn in the road, perhaps due to the darkness now settling around us, or perhaps we were all a bit tired.

Ballyheigue Castle had disappeared into the night by now and the Danish silver was safe once more.

Going on a Wild Ghost Chase

U SUALLY, WHEN I DECIDE TO INVESTIGATE A HAUNTED HOUSE, be it in America or abroad, I know exactly where it is located. I usually have been in contact with its owners or inhabitants by mail or telephone or both. But Ireland offers difficulties. The phone is of little use in the provinces. And as for the mail, how can you write to someone whose name you don't know at an address that may no longer exist?

I had taken a good look at the map and decided we should try and find Shallardstown. But nobody in Ireland ever heard of Shallardstown. To begin with, it's not a town but a house. What the Irish call a greathouse, a mansion. Long before we came to the Emerald Isle, I had read of Shallardstown in what is virtually the only source material on Irish ghosts—James Reynolds' marvelous book entitled *Ghosts in Irish Houses*. I had been given to understand from inquiries of the publishers—Reynolds died some years ago—that the stories in his books were factual and true, just as mine are. Consequently I felt it worth while to follow the trail of James Reynolds, and finish what he started, for Reynolds never took a medium of the likes of Sybil Leek with him when he roamed the Irish countryside in search of ghost stories. Of course, he himself was psychic and could "see things," but solo investigation is never the best way to investigate impartially and scientifically. Reynolds of course did not corroborate the material obtained psychically since he could not very well be investigator and medium at the same time.

The story of Shallardstown fascinated me on more than one account. Its eerie elements of violence and slow revenge were so typically Irish in their enduring hate; the total isolation of the place amid the Southern mountains sounded attractive, and the main character of the story was one Princess Orloff. Well, it so happens that my wife Catherine is the sixth generation descendant of a very famous couple—Catherine the Great of Russia and Prince Gregory Orloff, whose daughter Natalie went on to marry my wife's ancestor. Thus I had a personal motive, as well as a scientific one, in searching for the elusive Shallardstown.

My first source was of course Reynolds' account of Shallardstown, in which he traced the building of the greathouse, in the early 19th century, by Cadogan Parrott, who modelled the house after the Italian designer Andrea Palladio. In Reynolds' day—he completed the book in 1946—the house was still standing. Today it is an empty ruin. About that, later.

Here is how James Reynolds described this once magnificent mansion.

"Shallardstown stands deeply embowered in trees, mainly Irish oaks and beeches. It is a gracious house of soft white Connemara stone, not too large, but spacious. The flight of stone steps leading to the portico is a miracle of line and balance. The portico itself is one of the finest in Ireland. Inside the house are a series of living rooms opening one into the other in the Italian manner."

Incidentally, the name Shallardstown was given the house in honor of Cadogan's mother, whose maiden name was Shallard.

In 1806, Cadogan Parrott married a local woman named Angelica Gammage, according to Reynolds, and they had two girls, Angelica and Rosaleen. When the mentally disturbed mother died a suicide, Angelica the younger became mistress at Shallardstown. But her father also died soon after his wife, and now Angelica was the sole heiress to Shallardstown.

Reynolds goes on to report in colorful detail how Angelica Parrott had picked a handsome young man, Dagan Ferritter, to be her husband. She was rich and he was poor but it did not matter to her, for she wanted a healthy heir to Shallardstown and thought Dagan could give her just that. Unfortunately, the young man fell in love with her younger sister Rosaleen and married her instead of Angelica. This was 1837, and after the wedding the young couple left for the Continent on an allowance from Angelica. The following year, Angelica Parrott herself went abroad, and in London she met Prince Nicholas Orloff, first attaché at the Russian Embassy. They were married that year, and the following year, 1838, they returned to Paris from St. Petersburg, where Angelica had been a great success. Travelling in the winter was hazardous in those days, and Nicholas Orloff had caught a bad cold which cost him his life soon after. So it was that Angelica, now the Princess Orloff, returned to Ireland all by herself.

Immediately after her return to Shallardstown, she changed all servants, supervised now by a silent butler named Creed. The Princess never left the house, but the butler would go for provisions once in a while into the nearby villages of Clogheen and Ballymacorthy.

James Reynolds tells of the long-range vengeance Angelica had wrought on her sister and her husband, who was to be hers. Encouraging the man's innate idleness, she managed to have him pile up huge gambling losses until ultimately the young couple was forced to return to Ireland.

As she awaited their arrival, Princess Orloff started to take a daily ride in her landau at exactly the same time. She had her butler spread word that she was not well and would see no visitors. Every day at three, she would come out of the greathouse, holding a jewel encrusted whip, and drive through the countryside. It became such a daily routine, the people of the area took it in their stride like sundown or morning.

When the young couple arrived, Angelica refused to see them. They never spoke to her again. Except for a small monthly allowance, the sister and brother-in-law of the Princess were destitute. They lived in a small hut nearby, waiting for the day when Princess Orloff would die, leaving them sole heirs. But the years went by and the Princess would still be seen taking her daily ride in the countryside.

Finally, someone in a pub at Clogheen teased Rosaleen's husband into fury, telling him that the greathouse was rightfully his wife's. The next morning, Dagan and a crowd of villagers went up to the gates, which they found unlocked this time. They demanded to see the Princess. It was then that Creed, the butler, dropped the delayed action bomb.

The Princess had been dead for eleven years!

Creed, under orders from the Princess, had propped her body in the landau, holding the whip, so that for eleven long years a dead Princess had been seen riding around in the countryside. For eleven years the young couple had been living destitute, although the greathouse was theirs. That, according to James Reynolds, was Angelica's revenge on her sister and her faithless suitor.

There was a letter, dated May 12, 1861, in which she told of her inhuman plan shortly before she died. The letter was handed by Creed to the heirs. The whip, according to her wishes, had been placed in a glass showcase in the entrance hall. It was a souvenir of her happy days in Russia and she cursed anyone who dared touch it.

Dagan and Rosaleen finally took over Shallardstown, but both died within a year, too ill from their previous misfortunes.

The house passed into the hands of a cousin, and after that, in 1896, it became a Brothers Novitiate school. It was at that time that the first reports of ghostly goings-on were heard. Some of the boys and even teachers saw a shapeless figure in purple walk about the house and pause in front of the glass-enshrined Orloff whip, and moments later the sounds of a departing carriage were heard outside.

James Reynolds visited Shallardstown in 1937. The house

was neglected now and empty. Reynolds had made arrangements with an estate agent in nearby Clogheen to visit the house, and a Mrs. McArtagh, the caretaker, was there to greet him on that cold, windy day in February.

"I've heard footsteps on the stairs," the caretaker confided to Reynolds, "and twice I've seen a figure at the top of the stairs."

She thought that the devil was fooling around with the showcase in which the Orloff whip lay.

"Half the time I find the lid open—especially around four in the afternoon," she said to Reynolds.

He walked over to the case and opened it. When he touched the handle of the richly bejewelled whip, he found to his amazement that the handle was still warm—as if a human hand had recently held it. He glanced at his watch and found it was just after four o'clock. Had the ghost of Princess Orloff just returned from her customary afternoon ride?

So much for the James Reynolds story. There was nothing further I could find on Shallardstown or indeed the Parrott family, and I resigned myself to going "cold" after a haunted house for the first time in my ghost-hunting career.

*   *   *

Sylvester was our driver once again as we set out from the commodious accommodations of Dromoland Castle early in the morning, for the trip would be a long one and we wanted to be back in time for dinner. In time for dinner indeed! When our driver took a good look at the map, he shook his head in bewilderment. How could one drive that far and do all that in one day?

The beginning was easy enough. We took the main road to Tipperary, following pretty much the railroad through the rolling hills of County Limerick, and it wasn't a long, long way to Tipperary at all, for we passed through the old town in little more than two hours' time.

On we pressed towards Caher, where we had hoped to eat

lunch. Caher is a charming old town straddling a river called
Suir, with a ruined medieval castle on one side and a gleaming
white church on the other.

There being no suitable inn at Caher, I decided to combine
food with useful inquiry and stop instead at Clogheen, the
little town mentioned in James Reynolds' account. All along
the road we had encountered cattle, sometimes blocking the
right of way. But Sybil bailed us out of our difficulty. She had
been raised in rural England and knew the magic word—no
witchcraft here, just uf! uf!—and presto, the cows moved to
one side and let us pass.

We were coming into Clogheen now, and the land around us
took on more of a rugged appearance. Fewer houses and higher
ground surrounded the road, which also left much to be desired.
We were in the heart of southwestern Ireland now, just about
as far as one can be from the coast.

To our right, a fairly high mountain range called Galty
Mountains appeared, and we followed the winding road into
the little town called Clogheen. I made straight for the post
office, for in places of this size that is where all knowledge is to
be had.

The day before, I had telephoned the postmaster here, inquiring about Shallardstown. Neither he nor anyone else he consulted had ever heard of it or the Parrotts, which proves that
twenty-five years can indeed obliterate all knowledge even of
so great a house and so proud a family as the one we were
searching for.

Immediately, he realized who I was. Two people could not
possibly ask the same unanswerable question. He still had no
idea where either Shallardstown or Ballymacorthy was. It was
around one in the afternoon now and everybody was pretty
hungry. But the only inn around was filled up and could not
serve us, so we had to drive on. After a brief council of war I
decided that Ballymacorthy had to be somewhere on the other
side of the mountains that lay below Clogheen, judging again
from Reynolds' narrative. So we bravely set out on the winding

road that leads from Clogheen through the forbidding Knock-mealdown Mountains to Lismore and Cappoquin in County Waterford.

Of course I had no idea how high the mountains would turn out to be, or how difficult the road. We did have some provisions in the trunk of the car, but we preferred a hot meal.

Up and up it went, and soon the clouds came down and covered the road with clammy, moist air. We were driving right through them, high up on the mountain, and if ever I had a ghostly feeling on a road, this was it.

Way down through the mist we could see some of the lakes between the high peaks, but up ahead we could scarcely make out the road, despite the strong headlights Sylvester had turned on. It was getting towards two o'clock and I knew how difficult it is to get dinner in the countryside after the hour of two. But a short time later, we started to descend into the valley again. To our left, an almost invisible road went up to Mount Melleray monastery, a Trappist retreat where my two ladies would scarcely have been welcome. A little later we rolled into the sleepy little town of Cappoquin. There were two restaurants in town, and one did serve us, a reasonably good meal that fortified us for the search ahead. The local postmaster, who also doubled as grocery clerk—or rather, vice versa—was of no help at all, and we were told to try our luck in Dungarvan, on the South coast. There was a Ballymacorthy around there. It turned out to be Ballynacorthy, with an "n" instead of an "m."

Dungarvan, I was sure, was much too far south to be in the right area for us, but it was a fair-sized town and we should be able to get directions here at last. In the market square of this typically southern Irish town we saw a trailer staffed by the local Chamber of Commerce to help tourists find their way to the many attractions in which the area abounds. A dark-haired lady with a heavy southern flavor in her voice tried to help us. But all her books and maps were of no avail. Finally, Miss Eileen O'Flynn—you can't have a more Irish name than that—called in a friend, a teacher and historian by the name Cait Flynn, no relation, of course, and the second Miss Flynn was just as friendly and willing to help us as was the first. What's more, she had heard of *our* Ballymacorthy up in the mountains.

"You've come much too far south," she said, pointing at the area map. "Go back up to Clonmell and Caher, and then take the Banshire road and you'll get to Ballymacorthy."

She handed me her Automobile Club book with detailed maps that might help us find the elusive place.

"Keep it for good luck," she added, and I finally told her why we were looking for Ballymacorthy.

"The greathouse stands no more," she said, and my heart beat faster, for we had actually met someone who knew that there had been a greathouse. However, she had not heard the name Shallardstown. Then again, we were quite far from it and such a name given the house might have been known only in the immediate area.

I asked her about Ballymacorthy.

"It belonged to an Englishman, Sir Massey Dawson. He was an absentee landlord and during one of our 'troubles,' the house was largely destroyed."

"When was that?" I inquired. Reynolds had seen it still intact in 1937, and presumably, when his book was published in 1946, it was still intact or he would have altered his text to say it had been destroyed.

"In 1951," Miss Flynn replied.

Had she ever heard any ghost stories about the place?

Miss Flynn, a slight woman in her forties or late thirties, smiled.

"A cousin of mine, Jeremiah Maher by name, was with the I.R.A. in 1921. On one of their expeditions, they entered the greathouse, which was then empty. Jeremiah slept there that night, but he felt he was not alone in the room. He heard what he described as the grunting of pigs where there were no pigs. Noises in the night."

I thanked the two ladies and we set out for Clonmell. It was past four o'clock now and we would be arriving at the greathouse in time for sunset, but we had come thus far on a wild ghost chase, and I wasn't going to be done out of my ghost.

Somehow the road flew by faster now that we knew where we were going, and within an hour we passed through Clonmell, a clean, friendly town remarkable for the high spire of its cathedral. At Caher we turned into the right road instead of the wrong one we had taken earlier that day, and soon we found ourselves on a narrow country road where an encounter with a haywagon could mean endless delay.

The haywagon was not long in coming, but fortunately we were near a widening in the road, so we could bypass it. We kept asking and asking people for Ballymacorthy and counted side roads, for Miss Flynn had been explicit in telling us how to get there. It was six o'clock and the sun was getting low in the sky when we turned into a bumpy field road that was to bring us face to face with Ballymacorthy Greathouse.

No village nearby, only a couple of small houses, and, to our surprise, within the dilapidated gates, a modern two-story house barring the way up the main drive to the ruins of the greathouse. I later discovered that the land had been broken up and someone had bought part of it and put his house there. The main house was quite a distance from the gates; what there was of a drive was useless and the stairs were gone.

I began to wonder if we had really reached the right Ballymacorthy, for there was little resemblance between this ruin and the magnificent house so eloquently described by James Reynolds. Could a scant fifteen years create these desolate stone piles, overgrown by grass and plant life? Try as I would, I could not locate any other Ballymacorthy in the area. This was our place all right, but how it had changed.

We drove around the corner to the side gate to see if we could get in. The road was wet and one could hardly walk on it without sinking to one's ankles. We rounded the bend in the road and started up the other side of the wall. The wall was still intact, and a large metal gate barred entrance to strangers on the east end of the estate. Inside the gate, a lonely bull was grazing peacefully, and in the distance a few cows did likewise. The animals belonged to the farmer whose house we had passed earlier.

We left the car and made camp, so to speak. While Catherine prepared a small meal from what was originally meant to be our lunch, Sybil and I opened the heavy gates and explored. But there was nothing left but stone walls and not even a column indicating the once beautiful portico. No doubt the country people had long carted away whatever was useful elsewhere.

What had happened to the art treasures inside the house? What about the haunted Orloff whip Reynolds had still seen? In Ireland, these things have a way of disappearing in times of "trouble," which is nearly always. At least it was until a few years ago when the present Irish government finally brought peace and stability to the island. Today, the I.R.A. is dormant, if not extinct. But in the forties and even fifties, an English absentee landlord could never be sure if on returning to his greathouse in Ireland he would not be faced with a smouldering ruin.

Sybil meanwhile was walking around, completely unafraid of the bull. As she tried to gather what psychic impressions might be left in the ruins, I followed her about.

"I feel a great peace here," Sybil finally said, "and if there has been a ghost here it certainly has gone to rest now."

And so it was that our search for the ghost of Princess Orloff led only to a ruined greathouse she once called home.

ROOFTOPS OF DUBLIN

C. Budowski
6-66

The Ghosts in Dublintown

WE ARRIVED IN DUBLIN MINUS SYBIL LEEK, WHO HAD DECIDED to spend an extra day in the West at her friend's "castle." She was to join us later in the day at the Shelbourne Hotel. This hotel is not only the center of Irish literary and social life; it turned out to be haunted as well. The hotel's press representative, Una McNelis, left no closet unopened to find a spectre for us. Besides, she really made our stay at the Shelbourne all it should be.

We were given an apartment on the fourth floor whence we could look out over the rooftops of old Dublin and St. Stephen's Green below.

Shortly after our arrival, the telephone rang and Aidan O'Hanlan from the Tourist Board offered us the welcome of Dublin. He also informed us that he had arranged for a television interview and luncheon with a newspaper columnist and was it all right with us?

It was, and Sybil having meanwhile also arrived, we went to the local TV station and did our bit for Telefis Eireann the following day. Sybil and I sat with Brian Morrow and my ghost pictures, and the next day everybody recognized us from that appearance. As we walked down the quais looking at antiques we could hardly avoid the hellos of Dubliners with TV sets, of which there must be indeed many.

Catherine, independent soul that she is, filmed a talk with art critic Tom McConnery all by herself and that, too, was a success. Some of her paintings of haunted houses were shown on camera and everybody was suitably impressed. As for the columnist, he turned out to be charming, urbane Desmond Rushe of the *Independent*, who writes a column called "Tatler's Parade." We had a two-hour luncheon at the Shelbourne and Mr. Rushe's story brought me many new leads to haunted houses afterwards. Still another newsman had prepared the ground for our arrival. He was Patrick Byrne of the *Evening Herald*, who writes a regular column on ghosts. From his files of ghost lore, I was able to pick leads for possible investigations. Unfortunately, most of Mr. Byrne's material is legendary in character and good ghost stories rather than hard-core reports of contemporary hauntings.

That night, I called the television station to find out when our interview would be broadcast. I found out that in Ireland at least everything shuts down by evening.

"You mean, there is nobody around who can give me any information?" I said to the telephonist.

"Not a soul," she assured me.

"Then, pray, how do you run the station—with leprechauns?" I inquired, and she laughed a little uncertainly, but finally managed to find an editor who had stayed late and who was able to give me the information I wanted.

Speaking of leprechauns, and a lot of people do as soon as you mention Ireland, I do not claim to be an authority on the reality of Little People. But it is impossible to sweep under the carpet of reason all the reports that have been received on these very strange creatures. This has nothing to do with ghosts or even the psychic, since the Little People are evidently merely humans of small stature. But the reports persist. Back in 1958, when Shannon airport runways were being enlarged to accommodate bigger planes, the Irish contractor in charge of the work ran

afoul of a leprechaun or fairy settlement. Their fort was right in
the middle of the new runway. Ambrose McInerney, the contractor, was told not to move the earth at that spot. The aviation
engineers decided to reroute the runway rather than face a re-
bellious crew of workers—or worse. Superstition, you say?
Perhaps. But that's another book, some day, sometime.

Back at the Shelbourne, I received reports of haunted places
in and around Dublin. In New York already my friend and fel-
low-writer Elizabeth Byrd had told me of a certain house in
Fitzwilliam Street, where she had experienced a strange, psychic
smell. Would I go there and look? We went to number 12 Fitzwilliam Street, a beautiful Georgian townhouse in one of the
best parts of Dublin, but I smelled nothing—not even the gasoline
of the passing cars. Sybil, who never fails to pick up a ghost if
there is one around, also shook her head. No peppermint smell.
Whatever it was Elizabeth had experienced, it was not present
now.

We went down to St. Anne's Church in Dawson Street, where
two experiences had been reported to Patrick Byrne by a Mrs.
F. W. Gumley of Dublin. In one, a funeral had been taking place
in this Protestant church, with wreaths being placed on the
coffin during the services, when suddenly one of the wreaths
was clearly seen to move.

We sat in the ancient pews of this church and felt nothing.
Perhaps the incident was a passing one, someone not yet quite
dead trying to catch the eye of an interested party?

At any rate, I could not locate the witness and let the matter
drop.

Soon we found out that our hotel had a ghost that was not on
the program, so to speak. It all happened rather unexpectedly.

"As the Shelbourne is almost a hundred and fifty years old,
you may well find some inspiration for your book right here!"
Una McNelis had written me lightheartedly. She did not expect
me to be so successful, however.

The Shelbourne was founded in 1824, when Martin Burke
bought four brick houses, side by side, facing St. Stephen's

Green in what was then, and is now, one of the most elegant, yet central areas of Dublin. The houses were in the Georgian style of that period and they have remained untouched on the outside, although the inside of the hotel is modern and lacks none of the comforts associated with the 20th century. The 200 rooms differ greatly in style and layout, however, depending on floors and area, since, after all, four separate houses were brought together and connected by various corridors and staircases. In this respect it reminded me of the Savoy in London, which also has sections of varying backgrounds so that one may step from the eighth floor front directly onto the 11th floor.

We were located on the top floor, as I had asked for the quietest part of the hotel. The windows of most rooms here were smaller and the apartments had the appearance of an artist's garret, looking out over the rooftops of Dublintown very much like some of the Paris flats I've been in. It was quite obvious to me that the entire area had been servants' quarters at one time, for in old houses the lower floors are reserved for the master of the house, the walking of stairs being a privilege or rather a penalty of the serving classes.

Today of course there are up-to-date elevators at the Shelbourne, and the service is really excellent, so much so that it spoils you for other, less conscientious hotels and countries!

The morning after our arrival in Dublin, Sybil informed me that her room was haunted.

"Impossible," I said. "I've asked about any possible psychic business in the hotel and they assured me there was none."

"Well, there is," Sybil repeated in her usual factual way, and handed me her notes of the previous night. I had instructed her to take notes whenever anything unusual was happening and I was not around to do the recording myself.

"What exactly happened in room 526, Sybil?" I asked. The date was August 16, 1965.

"Well, I was doing some writing in the room and finally got to bed around 11 p. m. But I could not sleep, so I got up again and continued typing until 2:20 a.m. Then I returned to bed.

Lying awake, just thinking, I suddenly heard noises from the bathroom."

Room 526 is small and compact. There were a bed, a small desk, a couple of chairs, one large window facing St. Stephen's Green. The bathroom, partitioned from the room itself with a wood-and-glass partition, actually was within the room itself. Nobody could get into it except from the room. There was a tiny window in the outside of the bathroom but it was firmly closed from the inside.

"What did you think it was?" I asked.

"I thought it was a cat, and I listened again. This time I clearly heard a child crying. Not frantically, but steadily as if she had been crying for a long time and was getting tired."

"What did you do?"

"I called out, quite gently and not in fear at all—What's the matter? 'I'm frightened,' said a child's voice. 'Come to me then,' I said, still lying in bed. A few seconds later, I felt the foot of the bed being touched and then grasped as if some child were hauling itself onto the bed. Then a very small soft arm went around my neck. I felt the touch of a light woolly material across my right cheek and head and on my right outstretched arm.

"With that I fell asleep but woke up at 6:30, with my right arm still outstretched, when normally I sleep on my side. My right arm was numb until I had had a bath. Another strange thing—that night I was writing children's poetry, a thing I have never done in my life before, for I don't specialize in this type of writing."

I advised Sybil to try again the following evening and if the child made itself known again, to call me, or at the very least, ask some questions. I felt that the initial contact was a slight one and needed some reinforcement before I should attempt an investigation and possibly frighten the ghost away. For a child's ghost is a touchy thing and should not be approached quite so directly as an adult spectre.

On the 17th of August Sybil spent the evening chatting with Catherine, and I was busy arranging my notes for the next few days. At 11:30, Catherine returned to our apartment, which was located about seven or eight doors down the hall, on the same floor.

Right after Catherine left, Sybil fell asleep. She was awakened by the sound of material seemingly moving over the floor in the area of the bathroom. She put on the light and checked her watch. The time was 12:55. The street was noisy, what with constant movement of traffic, but what had awakened her was definitely a "small sound." Again, as on the previous night, her arm was stiff and she had been lying on her back.

There was a noise by the window, which she had left open, with the curtain drawn over it. It sounded like several knocks. She got out of bed and approached the window, when the curtain billowed out into the room twice and she suddenly felt very cold. The window, which she had left open, was now firmly closed! She opened it again and made sure it was secure.

Then Sybil sat down on the bed and wrote down in longhand what had just occurred. Immediately she became aware of a presence standing by her right knee and touching her right arm.

It was a small girl, about seven years old.

"I told her to go to bed," Sybil recalls. "She did—my bed!"

She got in over the foot of the bed and lay down on the right side. Sybil stopped writing and stared at her.

"Who are you?" she asked.

"I'm Mary Masters," the child said, but she did not want to talk, just appeared to be a very tired child. Sybil waited until she was asleep before writing again. The next morning she found she had written "1846," so that date must have had some significance in the matter.

At 1:30, Sybil got into bed herself, on the extreme left side, but the child moved towards her. She murmered something that sounded like—"Don't go, Sophie."

Well, Sybil did not go. Instead, she put her hand on the pillow and again felt the movement of some soft woolly material against her arm and face. But she slept, and her little companion did the same, because Sybil was able to sleep through to 7 a. m.

There the matter stood the following day, when Sybil reported it to me. I decided that we had better see what the little girl ghost wanted, and the following night Catherine and I joined Sybil at her room for a trance session.

"What did the little girl look like to you?" I questioned Sybil.

"She was as real to me as you are," Sybil said. "I could not see very much of the lower part of her body, I admit, but I have the impression of her face. She was not a particularly pretty child—she was a plain child."

"How was she dressed?"

"She had one garment on, and I think this was a woolen night shirt. She was obviously attired for bed."

"The name Mary Masters, which the ghost girl gave you, does it mean anything to you personally, I mean consciously?"

"Never heard it before."

Sybil then drew our attention to the general appearance of her room.

"Looks like a nursery, doesn't it?"

I confess it did, for the room was too small for an adult. I checked this out later with Una McNelis.

"I don't understand it," Miss McNelis admitted. "Why, that room was only added much later—thirty years ago it was made into what it is today, a small, single room."

What about the adjacent area?

"Oh, that," Miss McNelis explained, "that was part of the old Burke family house."

"Do we have any records as to previous owners, and unusual events during the nineteenth century?" I inquired, but Miss McNelis shook her head.

"Sorry," she said in her beautiful Dublin English which is so much clearer than British English, "but all the records were burned."

Nursery or servant's quarters, we had come to investigate the presence of a little girl ghost.

"I hope we can leave her happy," Sybil said. "You know I have a very soft spot for children in my heart—ghost or otherwise."

A moment later, Sybil was in deep trance on the bed. The

light to the right of her was burning, but we had turned the overhead illumination off. Catherine was tending to the tape recorder and from time to time we took photographs using only the available room light, very sensitive black and white film and long exposures.

After a few minutes, Sybil's face changed and an almost child-like expression came over her. A faint, weak voice tried to part her lips. I tried to ask her for her name, but she seemed to be too weak to speak as yet.

Finally, she whispered, barely audible, "Mary."

"Are you Mary?" I repeated.

"Mary Masters."

"How old are you?"

"Six."

"What is your father's name?"

"Timothy." I wasn't sure, but it sounded like it.

"Your mother's name?"

Again I could not be sure, for the voice was faint. But it sounded like "Anne."

Then the child added, of her own—"Sophie."

"Who is Sophie?"

"Plays with me."

"Is this your house?"

For a moment, the voice hesitated.

"I'm not going to talk to you."

I asked her what her father was doing.

"Working here," she replied and then added, "I'm going to bed."

She sounded like a petulant child. I asked if she was ill.

"I've got a bad cold—throat."

"Did the doctor take care of you?"

"Mama."

"Do you have any sisters and brothers?"

"Sophie . . . sister . . . big girl."

"Any others?"

"No."

"Who lives here?"

"Sophie . . . Mama . . . I want my mama!"

She was almost in tears now.

"What are you doing in this room?"

"My room."

"Are you doing something with the window?"

"Must not touch the window."

"Why?"

"Sophie throws things out."

"Were you in the bathroom just now?"

"I haven't had a bath for a long time."

"Do you have a nurse? A nanny?"

"No . . . she does not talk . . . Sophie. . . ."

Now the child started to hum.

I tried to tell her that her mama was waiting for her and she must go to her but the child refused.

"No . . . can't go . . . not down . . . must not go . . . Mama says not go . . . not go away from this room. . . ."

Heavy tears followed.

I started to send her away, gently and firmly. With a child ghost this requires a different technique from that used with an adult, of course. So I suggested she go to sleep and dream of her mama. After a while, the sobbing became less marked.

"Sleep with Sophie," the ghost mumbled. Evidently she had shared the bed, which was lately Sybil's, with her big sister Sophie.

A few moments later the voice was gone and Sybil came out of her deep trance, as always remembering nothing that had come from her entranced lips.

The name Masters could not be traced, at least not by me. Although the room itself had been created only thirty years ago, the area had been in use long before that. And long before the Georgian houses bought by Mr. Burke had been turned into Dublin's best hotel, there were houses on this busy spot.

So it stands to reason that somehow people lived here and died here, although their records may no longer be traced.

In 1846, the hotel was young and Ireland troubled. Could it then not be that so insignificant an event as a little girl's death from a bad cold could go unnoticed in the greater adventures of those perilous times?

*   *   *

Michael MacLiammoir is not only the premier actor of Ireland, but a gifted playwright, poet, producer and director, even a composer of music, and of course a boulevardier and, as they used to say, "a man of parts"—many parts. He is as well known to Broadway as he is at the Olympia and the Gate and indeed West End. When I appeared on Dublin TV, Brian Morrow told me of MacLiammoir's interest in the occult, and Patrick Byrne, the editor, had printed an interview with the great actor in which he told of his encounter with a ghost.

I decided I simply had to meet MacLiammoir, and meet him I did. He came over to the Shelbourne to have luncheon with Catherine and me, a most gracious man full of true modesty. After a good lunch—warm, of course—we repaired to our apartment upstairs for coffee. So highly respected is "Doctor MacLiammoir" in Dublin that the waiter did not dare come up for the dishes until well into the afternoon, out of fear of disturbing our conversation.

"Did you actually see a ghost?" I asked, when all was mellow, the coffee flowing freely, and the peaceful atmosphere of the apartment undisturbed by outside noise. Downstairs, we had not been able to talk more than politely, for the mixture of many voices and the clatter of dishes had created an atmosphere of restlessness around us. Here now all was calm, private.

"It begins in the year 1916, when I was a boy of sixteen. It was in the early spring, a month or so before the Rising of Easter Week 1916. I was reared in England as a boy and had been on the stage in the West End of London. Among the friends I met was a young man named Kenneth Dennis who, when war broke out, joined the British Army. And because of his religion—which was Catholic—but he had never set foot in Ireland and had nothing to do with it at all—he was given a commission in the Munster Fusiliers. He held the rank of captain.

"We were staying together on one of his reliefs from the front in France, during early March, staying at a very beautiful house of a friend, an 18th century house in a place called Isle-wyth on the river Thames. We shared a room in which we slept for three nights, and on the third night, the night before he was returning to France to fight, he was a little depressed and also exhilarated and I was merely inquisitive about ghosts. I was always interested in ghosts.

"That night he said convincingly to me that within three days after his return to France he would be dead. Heartless and young that I was, instead of being smitten with grief at the thought of death for my friend, I merely said, 'Do you promise, Kenneth, that you will come back and tell me?' I remember his face as he leaned on his elbow in his bed that was opposite mine and looked at me through the clouds of cigaret smoke and said, 'Yes, Michael, if God allows it, I will come back and tell you.'

"Three days later the news came back that he had been killed in some battle, and no ghost had appeared, no premonition even, nothing at all. I was griefstricken when I heard of his death, for he was a close friend, but being young and forgetful and on the whole heartless I forgot about him fairly soon. He went completely out of my mind.

"The scene passes now until twenty years later when I was well established back in my own country and had already met my present partner with whom I created in 1928 the Dublin Gate Theatre. And in the year 1936, before the Second World War, Hilton and I were sharing this apartment in Upper Mount Street in Dublin. It was a very pleasant apartment while we were waiting for a house to be furnished for us. We had just engaged a manservant who had excellent references but about whom I knew nothing at all except that he had been in the British Army and had good references from various military people.

"On the first morning of his duties with us, I woke up—a most unusual feat for me in those days—about five minutes to nine—nine o'clock was the call for us, for we had a ten o'clock rehearsal. I had instructed this new man to bring up the coffee, set it down and open the curtains, for the light coming into the room I knew would waken me.

"At five minutes to nine I remember waking up with a start and thinking, 'Oh what's wrong? Something is strange. Ah, it's nothing at all, merely that we've engaged a new manservant.'

"Presently I heard his step on the stairs, and looking at the clock, I thought, well, the man's punctual anyway—that's a wonderful thing in Ireland and I was delighted. Very softly, very discreetly the door opened, and to my astonishment, in the dim light that was filtering through the curtains of the room, I *saw a British officer*, a tall, smartly dressed British officer with light brown hair, carrying a tray. Looking very fine and elegant, he carried the tray into the room and then did the most unexpected thing—he closed the door of the room with his backside, which did not seem to me in keeping with the rest of him, and I wondered what in the name of heaven a British officer was doing in Dublin in the year 1936.

"And suddenly I realized who it was. My old friend Kenneth Dennis. Not startled but certainly not frightened, but filled with undescribable emotion, I sat up and said—'Kenneth! It is Kenneth Dennis, it's you, Kenneth?'

"The officer nodded his head, still carrying his coffee tray, moved around the bed, still with his eyes fixed on me, his mouth moving as though he were speaking to me though I could hear no word at all. But I saw him plainly and solidly—he was just a British officer carrying a tray of coffee. He set the tray down on my bed, and still with his eyes fixed on me he went to the curtains and drew them open; and the dull, gray light of an early March morning in Ireland streamed into the room.

"And as it illuminated this figure at the window, the figure of the officer had been replaced by a curious sort of process that I can't describe—and I saw in place of the smartly dressed and well-groomed officer standing there an elderly man, in a white coat and black trousers, still drawing the curtains open. I looked at him in astonishment and saw that the man's face was white and he seemed pretty much shaken.

" 'And what is wrong with you?' I asked.

" 'Oh, I'm sorry, sir,' he said, 'but didn't I hear you say a name just now—a name Kenneth Dennis?'

" 'Yes, he was a very old friend of mine,' I said matter-of-factly. 'I was dreaming and—'

" 'Was it *Captain* Kenneth Dennis, sir?'

" 'It was.'

" 'And was he in the Munster Fusiliers, sir?'

"I said, yes, that was his regiment.

" 'Oh my God,' he said, 'I knew him—I was Captain Dennis' batman. He died in my arms. In France, in 1916.'

"That was all."

For a minute or two, we all sat in silence, pondering what we had just heard.

"Did you feel it was a ghost at the time?" I finally asked Michael MacLiammoir.

"I could not describe my feelings at the time, for the whole thing was rapid—less than a minute. The man himself I afterwards discovered by various other smaller incidents was what you would call a natural medium. An untrained, natural medium, as many of our country people in Ireland are.

"He was a Sligo man from the West of Ireland. He had that strange quality that made him hear voices at times, see spirits, and occasionally know what was in a letter before it arrived or he would know that something was coming. For example, on another occasion, he came into our room one day in the same house and said, 'The telegram you're expecting arrived, sir, and you'll be off to America soon.'

" 'What telegram?' I said.

" 'Here,' he said and held out his empty hand, and I said— 'There is no telegram—what are you talking about?'

" 'My God,' he finally said, 'what did I do with that? I must have dropped it somewhere. But I had a telegram for you and it was from America, asking you to go out there. And you'll go all right.'

"I said, 'But where is the telegram?'

"At that moment, there was a loud rap at the door. There was a telegraph boy there standing with a telegram. And sure enough it was from my old friend Orson Welles inviting us for a summer stock season in Illinois."

Again, there was a pause.

"Have you had other experiences before the incident with the ghost of the British officer?" I asked.

"Many," Michael MacLiammoir replied. "All through my life I've had minor experiences."

"Have you ever gone into a house and felt strange because of the atmosphere in it?"

"Very frequently. Only a couple of months ago I was playing in the city of Galway, in the West of Ireland. We were invited to luncheon one day by a man we hardly knew, and his wife, very charming people. We went, and as he went to show me his most beautiful and interesting factory that was near his house—of Irish porcelain—suddenly crossing the yard I said to my manager, who was with me, 'There is a woman walking through this place who is not of this earth, and with her is a dog.' And he looked at me if I were quite crazy, for he is not particularly interested in such things. He spoke of it to the owner, who confessed that the place was supposed to be haunted by a woman who had been murdered there, years before, and that there was a dog who tried to protect her."

I secretly regretted not having known about this case when we had been in Galway City a few days prior to our Dublin visit.

"Oh and in Edinburgh," MacLiammoir continued, "the room I was put asleep in in a small hotel when I was playing the Edinburgh Festival—I could not stay in the room. Because I was conscious in the bed of great physical anguish. A woman in great distress. I was told afterwards that someone had died in childbirth in that bed. Those things happen to me frequently.

"Another time, on the journey back from America, in golden October, right across the Atlantic—I was walking around the ship—it was in 1934 and I had gotten up particularly early, although we had worked hard the day before.

"I was walking round and round the deck. Slowly I heard someone singing in my ears, an old French song—I hadn't heard it for years and it was called '*Le baiser.*' It was a girl's voice and suddenly I recognized the voice as my sister's.

"Slowly I became aware that she was walking around the deck with me. We walked round and round, and I began singing the song myself. I was extraordinarily happy, for I hadn't seen her for many years. She was a sister I loved very much.

"I did not know, but *it was at that moment that she died!*

"When I got home to Ireland five days later, I was met by my aunt and she said, 'I'm terribly sorry, but I've sad news for you,' and we traced it back and it was that morning when she died."

Meanwhile it was almost four in the afternoon and the busy actor-producer was 'way overdue at a conference. But I don't think he regretted our meeting any more than I did, and outside the door to our apartment, the waiters were standing almost at attention when he left. For such is the strange climate of Ireland that a man can believe in ghosts and be highly respected for it.

SKRYNE CASTLE
IRELAND

C. BUXKIVEDEN
8-66

The Ghosts at Skryne Castle
and the Windswept Hills of Tara

ONE FINE DAY WE STARTED OUT FROM DUBLIN ABOARD ONE of the Murray cars one rents in Ireland if one doesn't have a car of one's own, and as luck would have it, we had a most pleasant and intelligent driver by the name of Guy Crodder, who understood immediately what we were after.

Passing the airport, we started to look for Mara Castle, a ruin James Reynolds had briefly mentioned in his Irish ghost books as being suspect from the ghost-hunting point of view. The suburban town of Newton-Swords was interesting and charming, but nobody there knew of Mara Castle. Since our schedule for the day was heavy, I decided to go farther north. We took some of the quiet back roads, but our driver had a good sense of direction, and by high noon we had arrived at our first destination.

County Meath is much less forbidding than the West of Ireland we had recently left, and the nearness of the river Boyne gave the land an almost Southern charm. Before us rose majestically the high tower of a ruined church, built in the 14th century and dedicated to St. Colmcille, one of Ireland's three most sacred saints. The tower, sixty feet high on a hill of about 500 feet elevation, dominates the landscape. But it was not this once magnificent church we were seeking out. The much smaller castle of Skryne or Screen, at the foot of the hill, was our goal.

What had brought me here was a brief story in James Reynolds' *More Ghosts in Irish Houses*, published in 1956. He tells of this castle, smallish as castles go, set back of the river Boyne woodlands, not far from Tara, which he visited when it was owned by a relative of the Palmerston family which had long owned the house.

According to Reynolds, the tragedy that led to the haunting at Scryne happened in 1740. At that time the occupants of the house were one Sir Bromley Casway, and his ward, a beautiful young girl by the name of Lilith Palmerston. Lilith had led a sheltered life here and in Dublin, and had had little contact with the world of society or men. During her long stay at Skryne, she met a country squire named Phelim Sellers whose house stood not far from Skryne and whose wife had died mysteriously, possibly as the result of a beating administered by the brutish man.

Lilith Palmerston instantly disliked the neighbor. He in turn became a frequent visitor at Skryne Castle, playing cards with her elderly guardian, but always having an eye for her. On one occasion, Reynolds tells us, Sellers attacked her but was thwarted in his design by the gardener. Now Lilith asked that they return to Dublin to escape the unwanted attentions of this man. Her guardian agreed and all was in readiness for their journey down to the city. The last night before their planned departure, Sellers got wind of Lilith's plans, broke into her room and murdered her. Later caught, he was hanged at Galway City.

A number of persons living at the castle have heard shrieks in the night, and seen a woman in white clutching at her throat run out of the house.

Sellers had killed Lilith by forcing foxglove fronds down her throat, thus strangling her.

So much for Reynolds' vivid account of the tragedy at Skryne Castle.

I had not announced our coming, but we were fortunate in

that the castle was open. It so happened that the owners were tossing a wedding breakfast for someone in the area; thus the house was bustling with servants. It was even more fortunate that only the downstairs part of the old house was being used for the festivities, leaving us free to roam the upper stories at will.

The house stood across from a cluster of very old trees, and on the meadow between them a lonely goat tended to her luncheon.

Built in 1172, the castle had fallen into disrepair and was rebuilt in the early 19th century. I walked around the castle, which looked more like an early Victorian country house than a castle, despite its small tower rising above the second story. The house was covered with ivy from one end to the other. The windows were neat and clean and the garden in back of the house seemed orderly.

I managed to talk to one of the caterers in the house, a lady who had come here on many occasions and slept upstairs now and then. She was Kay Collier, and quite willing to talk to me even about so elusive a subject as ghosts.

"I've never noticed anything unusual myself," she began, "but there is a tradition about a ghost here. It's a tall man walking around with a stick, wearing a hard hat, and a dog with him. He's been seen outside the castle. Mrs. Reilly, of Skryne, she's seen him."

Since she could not tell us anything more, I made a mental note to look up Mrs. Reilly. Then I asked Sybil, who had been sitting quietly outside under the age-old tree, to join Catherine and me in the upstairs rooms of the castle. The salon to the left of the stairs was elaborately and tastefully furnished in early Victorian style, with mirrors on some of the walls, delicate furniture, couches, sofas and small antiques dressing up the room.

Sybil sat down in one of the comfortable chairs, placed her hand over her eyes and gathered impressions. For a moment, no one spoke. The silence, however peaceful on the surface, was forbidding, and there was, to me at least, an atmosphere of doom hanging rather heavily around us in this room.

"This room immediately attracted me," Sybil said now.

"You know I first turned right, then turned around and came straight to this room instead."

I nodded. She had indeed changed course as if led by some invisible force.

"I feel that this is where a woman has walked," Sybil said slowly, deliberately. "The mirrors have some significance; perhaps there was a door behind the mirror on the right hand side, because she comes from the right. Whether she comes from the garden. . . ."

Was Sybil making contact with the unlucky wraith of Lilith whose favorite spot the garden had been, the same garden where her battered body had been found?

Naturally I had never told her of the tradition surrounding the castle, nor of James Reynolds' account.

"Do you feel her now?" I asked.

"Very slightly," Sybil replied, and looked up. "I don't think that she has been seen for some time. Fifty-eight, fifty-nine. I don't think she has made her presence known for some time, *but she is here.*"

"Can you communicate with her?"

"I'm only conscious of her, but not directly in contact with her. Also, there seem to be two periods, and yet the woman should not be a 'period piece' ghost—and yet she has this link with the past."

"What period do you think she belongs to?"

"I have an early period, of 1624, but the feeling in this room is of a very feminine influence, two periods."

"What did you feel outside the castle?"

"The tree is very important to this house somehow."

"What did you feel by the tree?"

"There I felt conflict. There I felt death. A man. This is the early period. We should go back to the tree, I think."

"Anything else you feel here?"

"I think something happened here in 1959. Perhaps the lady walked. I think you will find a link, something running, not from the house but to the house. That's where the tree comes in. Running from the old place, the church tower to this house— not this house but the one that stood here then."

"Can you describe any figure you see or sense?"

"Here the woman I see has fair hair, arranged in curls; she belongs to the early 1900's—twenty-two comes up—I keep seeing the number 22. Could be her age. Perhaps she is a descendant of the people in the yard."

"Any names?"

"I have the girl's name . . . there are two names . . . Mathilda, Mary . . . Madeleine . . . *Mathild* . . . something like that. . . ."

Was Sybil referring to Lilith? How close are the sounds of Lilith and Mathild? Was she repeating a whispered name from the faint lips of a long-ago murder victim?

We left the room now and walked to the tree opposite the castle. Here Sybil sat down again and listened to what her psychic sense would tell her. The tree must have been here centuries ago and its twisted, scarred branches must have witnessed a great deal of history.

"What do you get, Sybil?" I finally asked.

"This is connected with the early part of the house. As I see it, the original drive to the house would be just in front of this tree. Coming down the rough driveway I have the distinct feeling of a horseman. Sixteenth century. He is running away from soldiers, running to this house. The soldiers are not Irish. There is a foreign element here."

"Is the one who is running Irish?"

"He is not Irish, either. But he belongs to this area. The soldiers following him have nothing to do with the area. They're alien. This is the remnant of a battle. He is taking refuge, but he does not reach the house."

"What happens to him?" I asked.

"His stomach is injured. The soldiers come down to the house. His body is near this tree. The injury is because of a horse going over him, I think, and he is left here. He dies here—he does not reach the house."

"Is he a soldier or a civilian?"

"I think he is a civilian, but who is to know in these times. . . ."

"Anything about a name, or rank?"

"I only get a foreign name. It's a French-Italian name. Alien to this country although he lives here."

"Is he still here under this chestnut tree?"

"Yes, he is," Sybil replied. "He still has to reach the house; he is not aware that he is dead. He has the feeling he has to get to the house. But he can't do it."

"Does he wish to talk to us?"

"He has someone close to him, not a blood relation, perhaps a brother-in-law, in the house. This is the person he had to go to. Fian . . . F-I-A-N-M-E . . . Fianna. . . ."

"Anything we can do for him?"

"I think that he would have to have some relation here, he has to feel a link. To know that he can go to the house. He is bewildered."

"Tell him the house has changed hands, now belongs to a Mr. Nichols," I said, but Sybil shook her head, indicating the futility of communication at this point.

"It was a much bigger house, much rougher house," Sybil said, and of course the original Skryne castle was all that.

"A much straighter house," Sybil continued to describe what she saw in the past, "with the door more to the right than it is now. The door he is heading for. The little garden was part of the house."

I asked Sybil to reassure the ghost that we would help him.

Sybil told the ghost that he was safe from his pursuers, and not to worry about reaching the house.

"Now he is to my right," Sybil said, and a moment later, "I can't find him now. I can only hear this one word—FIANMA—"

I promised to deliver the message, whatever it meant, for him, and suddenly the ghost was gone.

"He's gone now," Sybil said quietly, "and now the house is gone."

We packed up and started back to the village of Skryne, to look for Mrs. Reilly.

Much later I consulted the material about Skryne and I found some interesting information.

A local historian, the Reverend Gerald Cooney, wrote:

"The ancient name of Skryne was Ochil or Cnoc Ghuile, meaning the Hill of Weeping. Following the death of Cormac mac Airt, who established the *Fianna*, his son Cairbre became Highking. The Fianna rebelled against their king and the battle of Gabhra (Gowra) was fought at the foot of the hill now called Skryne. The Fianna were utterly defeated but Cairbre was killed in the battle."

The Fianna were the partisans of parliamentary government in medieval Ireland. Had Sybil somehow mixed up her centuries and seen a ghost going back to this battle?

We did not have to drive far. Someone pointed Mrs. Reilly's house out to me and I walked down a little country road to her gate. The house was set back behind a well-kept wall, a neat, reasonably modern country house covered by flowers. I rang the bell at the gate and soon enough Mrs. Reilly came out to greet me. She was a spunky lady in her sunny years, and quite willing to tell me all about her ghostly experiences.

"I can't exactly tell you when it happened," she said with a heavy brogue, "but it was a long time ago. I know about it through an uncle of mine, also named Reilly. I'm Kathleen Reilly."

"What is the story then?" I asked. The Irish have a way of telling someone else's story and sometimes a lot gets lost in the transition—or added. I wanted to be sure the account was believable.

"The ghost, well he was a coachman, and he had a dog. He was seen several times about the castle. And then there was a ghost of a nun seen, too."

"A nun?" I asked.

"A long time ago, the castle was a monastery and there was a nun's room."

"Was there ever any battle around here?"

"The battle of Tara," she replied and pointed towards another hill. "That's Tara over there."

"Has anyone ever come from there and taken refuge in the castle?"

"Not that I ever heard of."

She took me up to the house where I could see across the wooded glen to Skryne Castle.

"You see the spire?" she asked. "Well, right underneath is the nun's room."

The room Sybil had felt the woman's presence in, I realized at once.

"Twenty years ago," Mrs. Reilly volunteered, "a man I know by the name of Spiro slept in that room. He saw the nun, and he would never go back into that room."

"Did anyone ever die violently in the castle?"

She was not sure. The house had been in the same family until 25 years ago when the present owner, Nichols, bought it.

"The girls often heard noises . . . the rustling of clothes. . . . I thought I heard footsteps there one night when I was sittin' for the woman who has it now. I did hear footsteps, and there was no one in to my knowledge but myself."

"Where in the house was that?" I asked.

"The part where the nuns are supposed to be there," Mrs. Reilly replied. In other words, the upstairs salon where we had been, which was Lilith's room.

"Have you been there often?"

"Many times. I worked there three years."

"Are you ever afraid?"

"No, I'm not. When I heard the footsteps I was a bit afraid, but it went away."

I thanked Mrs. Reilly and pondered the business about the nuns. Had the witnesses merely drawn on their knowledge of a monastic background of the house to ascribe the rustling of clothes to nuns? Had the figure in a white bed robe seemed like a nun to them? And was it really Lilith's ghost they had encountered?

Puzzle upon puzzle.

Our driver suggested that we drive into the nearby town of

Navan, also known in Gaelic as An Uaimh. Here we found a nice restaurant and had a warm meal. The hills of Tara were our next goal, and though I had no reason to suspect a haunting in Ireland's ancient capital, or what was left of it, I nevertheless felt it was a worthwhile excursion. One could always try to see if Sybil got any impressions. Enough mayhem had taken place here over the centuries to create disturbances.

We arrived on the hill where Tara once stood in little more than half an hour. The place is absolutely breathtaking. Except for a hut where a small entrance fee is paid to this national shrine, and a church on a tree-studded hill in the distance, the hill, or rather the hilly plateau, is completely empty. Ancient Tara was built mainly of wood, and not a single building is now above ground.

Here and there a bronze plaque on the ground level indicates where the buildings of the old Irish capital stood. Brian Boru held court here in the 11th century, and after him, the office of Highking fell into disrepute until foreign invaders made Ireland part of their domain.

As we looked around, the wind howled around us with unabating fury. The view was imposing, for one could look into the distance towards Dublin to the south, or towards Drogheda to the north, and see the rolling hills of Eastern Ireland.

"I don't think I have ever been so moved by a place since I was in Pompeii," Sybil said. "The tremendous Druidic influences are still around and I wish this place were kept in a better state so that people could come here and see it as it was."

As an archaeologist, I could only concur with Sybil. The ominous shapes under the soil surely should be excavated. But I learned that only part of the land on which Tara once stood was owned by the nation; a small portion of it was privately owned and therein lies so much of Ireland's trouble: they could not get together to allow for proper excavations, so none took place.

The Ghost of the Olympia Theatre

THERE ARE THREE THEATRES OF RENOWN IN DUBLIN: THE GATE, the Abbey and the Olympia. The Gate is currently closed for repairs, and the Olympia was running a musical revue when we visited Dublin for the first time, in the late summer of 1965.

Lona Moran, the stage designer, had first told me of the hauntings at the Olympia, and my appetite was further whetted by Michael MacLiammoir, although he thought the Gate's ghosts were more impressive!

We booked seats for the night of August 19th. The revue starred popular Irish comedian Jack Cruise in something called "Holiday Hayride." To tell the truth, it was pleasant without being great, and we laughed frequently at what to sophisticated Americans must have appeared old-hat comedy. Overtones of Palace vaudeville made the show even more relaxing and the absence of boisterous rock and roll groups—inevitable in England these days—made it even nicer for us. In a comedy sketch taking off on Dublin police—called here the Garda—one of the cops played by Chris Curran made reference to our TV appearance that morning, proving again how small a town Dublin really is. Or how topical the revue was. At any rate, Lona Moran, who had often worked here before becoming the designer for Telefis

Eireann, had arranged to meet us after the show and discuss the haunting with us.

Dick Condon, the house manager, joined us in the bar around eleven, and Miss Moran was not long in coming either. Sybil's purple evening sari drew a lot of attention, but then Sybil is used to that by now.

We decided to repair to the stage itself, since the house had meanwhile gone dark. The stagehands agreed to stay a little late for us that night, and I started my inquiry.

"I've heard some very curious tappings and bangings," Lona Moran began, "and doors being shaken when they were very heavily chained. I have heard windows rattle, outside the room where I was sitting, and when I came out I realized there was no window!"

"How long ago was that?"

"That was about this time last year," Lona Moran replied. "It was in the backstage area, in the dressing room upstairs, number 9. Outside there is a completely blank wall. Actually, Mr. O'Reilly was with me and he heard it too. It was early morning when I went into that room, about half past five. We had been working all night. We went up to the dressing room to make notes and also to make tea, and this awful banging started. It sounded like a window being rattled very, very persistently. I went stiff with fright. I was very tired at the time. At intervals, the noise covered a period of about an hour, I'd say, because we left the room around 6:30 and only then we realized there was no window."

"Did you hear this noise at any other time?"

"Yes, when I worked on stage during the night. I heard a window rattle, and once got as far as the first floor to see if I could see it and then I lost my nerve and came down again."

"There was no possibility of a window making the noise?"

"Well, I suppose a window could have done it—but *what window?*"

"Do you know if any structural changes have taken place here?"

"No, I don't; but the theatre is over two hundred years old."

"Do you know if any tragedy or other unusual event took place in this area?"

"I don't know of any, but the theatre is supposed to be haunted. By what, I really don't know."

"Did you experience anything unusual before last year?"

"Yes, before then there were lots of bangings. The door of the bar would shake and rattle very badly, on very calm evenings, as if someone were rattling it. The sound of things dropping also. I thought Jeremy, my assistant, was dropping things and accused him rather sharply, but he wasn't."

"Ever hear footsteps?"

"I think I've imagined I heard footsteps—I don't know really whether they were or weren't—always during the night when we were working—two of us would be working on the stage together, and no one else in the theatre."

"And what happened on those occasions?"

"Rattling noises and creaking . . . and something that might be footsteps."

"Have you ever felt another presence?"

"I had the feeling last September that there was something there, when I walked through that door and saw no window."

I asked if she had ever had psychic experiences before she set foot into the theatre.

"I simply did not believe, but I do now," Lona Moran replied. She had never experienced anything unusual before coming to the Olympia. She had worked as stage designer for the Olympia Theatre for fourteen months prior to going into television.

I turned to Lona Moran's associate, who had come along to tell of his own experiences here.

"My name is Alfo O'Reilly," the tall young man said, "and I'm theatre designer and television designer here in Dublin. I myself have designed only two or three productions here, and last year, for the theatre festival, I designed an American production. On the particular evening in question Lona and I worked very late into the night, and I had not heard any stories at all about this theatre being haunted. We went up to the dressing room, and we were sitting there quietly exhausted when we heard these incredible noises."

"Those are the noises Miss Moran spoke of," I commented, and Alfo O'Reilly nodded and added:

"I have found that when I'm terribly exhausted, I seem to have a more heightened awareness. We knew there was only one other person in the theatre, the night watchman who was roaming elsewhere, and we were alone upstairs. There was certainly nothing in the corridor that could create this kind of noise. I've heard many things, footsteps, at the Gate Theatre, which is certainly haunted, but not here."

I thanked Mr. O'Reilly and turned to a slim young man who had meanwhile arrived onstage.

"My name is Jeremy Swan and I work with Telefis Eireann," he said by way of introduction, "and I used to work here as resident stage manager. About this dressing room upstairs—I remember one season here, during a pantomime, the dressing room was wrecked, allegedly by a poltergeist."

"Would you explain just how?"

"All the clothes were strewn about," Swan explained, "makeup was thrown all around the place—we questioned all the chorus girls who were in the room at the time—that was number 9 dressing room."

The haunted dressing room, I thought.

"Apparently there had been knocking at the door every night and nobody there," the stage manager continued, "at half past nine. One night when I was working here as assistant to Miss Moran I went upstairs to the washroom there, and when I came out I felt and I was almost sure I saw a light—just a glow—yellow; it seemed to be in the corner of the corridor. I followed the light round the corner—it moved, you see—and it went into the corridor where number 9 was, where there was another door. The door was open, and now it closed in my face!"

"Incredible," I was forced to say. "What happened then?"

"There was nobody in the theatre at all. It was after midnight. Now all the doors in the corridor started to rattle. That was four years ago."

"Have you had any experiences since then?"

"I haven't worked here very much since."

"Did you feel any unusual chill at the time?"

"Yes, I did before I went upstairs to the corridor. It was very cold onstage. Suddenly, I heard whispering from back in the theatre."

"What sort of whispering?"

"Sh-sh-sh-sh," Jeremy Swan went on. "It sounded like a voice that didn't quite make it."

"Anything else?"

"Then I heard this banging again. Beside me almost. On stage. I did not want to say anything to Miss Moran, and then I went up to the washroom where this funny light business started."

"At what height did the light appear?"

"Sort of knee level."

I thanked the young man and looked around. The stagehands had come forward the better to hear the questioning. Somehow they did not mind the overtime; the subject was fascinating to them.

All this time, of course, Sybil Leek was absent, safely out of earshot of anything that might be said about the haunting onstage. I was about to ask that she be brought in to join us, when a middle-aged stagehand stepped forward, scratched his head and allowed as to some psychic experiences that might perhaps interest me.

"What is your name, sir?" I asked the man.

"Tom Connor. I'm an electrician. I've been here fifteen years."

"Anything unusual happen to you here at the Olympia?"

"About eight years ago when I was on night duty here, I heard footsteps coming down the stairs. So I thought it was one of the bosses coming and I went to check and there was nobody, so I went to the top of the house and still didn't see anybody.

I came back again and I heard footsteps coming down the gallery, so I went to the switchboard, put on the house lights and searched—but there was nobody there."

"Did you hear this just once?"

"During the same fortnight when that show was on," Tom Connor replied quietly, "I had the same experience again. Footsteps coming down from the dressing rooms. I went and checked. Still, nobody. Couple of nights afterwards, I was having a cup of tea, and I was reading a book, sitting on the rostrum, and the rostrum lifted itself a few inches off the ground! I felt myself coming up and I thought it was one of the bosses, and I said, well, I'm awake! It's all right, I'm awake. But to my surprise, there was nobody there."

"You felt the rostrum physically lifted up?"

"Yes, as if someone of heavy weight had stood on the end of it."

"So what did you do then?"

"When I realized that there was no one there, I got a shock and felt a cold shiver, and put on more lights and had a look around. There was nobody in the theatre."

"Did you ever experience anything unusual in the area of the dressing rooms upstairs?" I asked.

"No, except that I heard the footsteps coming down, very clearly."

"Man or woman?"

"Heavy footsteps, like a man's."

"Anything else?"

"Well, at night, half past twelve, one o'clock, I get this cold, clammy feeling—my hair standing on end—I am always very glad to get out of the place."

Meanwhile, Dick Conlon, the house manager, had come onstage, having finished counting his money for the night.

I interrupted my interesting talk with Tom Connor, stagehand, to question Conlon about his experiences, if any, at the Olympia.

"I've been here thirteen months," he said, "but so far I haven't noticed anything unusual."

By now Sybil Leek had joined us.

"Sybil," I said, "when we got to this theatre earlier this evening, you did not really know where we were going. But when we got to our seats in stage box 1, you said to me, 'Something is here, I feel very cold.' What was your impression on getting here?"

"There is undoubtedly a presence here and I think it moves around quite a lot. The box has some association with it. I am mainly concerned though with the dressing room that had the number changed. I have not been up to this room, but it is upstairs. Second door, almost faces the stage. The corridor continues and there is a left hand turn. Then there are two doors. Not a particularly healthy presence, I feel. *I don't feel it is connected with the theatre.*"

"Then how would it be here?"

"I have an impression that this is something in the year 1916, and something very unruly, something destructive. It is a man. He doesn't belong here. He wishes to get away."

"What is he doing here?" I asked. The story was taking a most unusual turn.

Sybil thought for a moment as if tuning in on her psychic world.

"He stayed here and could not get out, and the name is Dunnevan. That is the nearest I can get it. I can't see him too well; the clearest place where I see him is upstairs, along the corridor that faces the stage on both landings. Near the dressing room that had the number changed."

"This man—is he a soldier or a civilian?" I asked.

"There is so much violence about his nature that he could have been of military character. But again I get a little confusion on this."

"Did he die here?"

"I have a feeling that he did, and that he came to a very un-

savory end. Perhaps not within the walls of this place, but having been here, having stayed here for some time. I think he
wanted to stay in here. After the theatre was closed."

"Is there any fighting involved?"

"Yes, I have the feeling of some violence. More people than
this man."

"Is he alone?"

"*He is the victim of it.*"

"What does he want?"

"I think he just is continuing in the same violent way in which
he lived."

"Why is he causing these disturbances?"

"He needs to escape. A connection with . . . I think this man
has sometime been imprisoned. The noises are really his protes-
tation against the periods of being restricted. He does not know
this is a theatre. But something vital happened in that top dressing room and the impressions there would be clearer."

Unfortunately, the hour was so late we could not go up there
that night.

"This man moves around the theatre a lot," Sybil commented.
"He was moving around here under pressure."

I thanked Sybil, and not knowing if any of the material obtained from her in this clairvoyant state had validity, I looked
around for someone who could either confirm or deny it.

Again, a stagehand, Albert Barden, was helpful.

"There was some fighting here," he said in his deliberate voice.
"It was during the Easter rebellion, in 1916."

"Any soldiers here?" I asked, and a hush fell over the audience
as they listened to the stagehand.

"As a matter of fact," he continued, "there was a civilian shot
—he was suspected of I.R.A. activities, but it was discovered
afterwards that he had something to do with the Quartermaster
stores down in Ironbridge Barracks. *He was shot by mistake.*"

"Where was he shot?"

"In the theatre."

"Downstairs?"

The man nodded.

"Though I was only six years old in 1916, I remember it as if it were yesterday. It was sometime between the rebellion and the Black and Tan fighting of 1921, but he surely was shot here."

In Ireland, it is sometimes difficult to distinguish between the two civil wars; as a matter of fact, they run one into the other, for it is true that for five long years all of Eire was a battleground for freedom.

It was very late by now and we had to leave the theatre. Outside, Dublin was asleep except for a few pubs still plying their trade.

I thanked Lona Moran and her friends for having come down to help us pin down the spectre of the Olympia.

Now at least they know it isn't a fellow thespian unhappy over bad notices—but a man who gave his life in the far grimmer theatre of reality.

RENVYLE HOUSE HOTEL
CONNEMARA

C. Burlingden
8-66

Renvyle

ALL ALONG THE IRISH COUNTRYSIDE, WHENEVER I GOT TO TALK about ghosts, someone mentioned the ghost at Renvyle. Finally, I began to wonder about it myself. In Dublin, I made inquiries about Renvyle and discovered that it was a place in the West of Ireland. Now a luxury hotel, the old mansion of Renvyle in Connemara was definitely a place worth visiting sometime, I thought. As luck would have it, the present manager of the Shelbourne in Dublin had worked there at one time.

I immediately requested an interview with Eoin Dillon, and that same afternoon I was ushered into the manager's office tucked away behind the second floor suites of the hotel.

Mr. Dillon proved to be an extremely friendly, matter-of-fact man, in his early middle years, impeccably dressed as is the wont of hotel executives.

"I went to Renvyle in 1952," he explained, "as manager of the hotel there. The hotel was owned originally by the Gogarty family, and St. John Gogarty, of course, was a famous literary figure. He had written a number of books; he was also the original Buck Mulligan in Joyce's *Ulysses*, and he was a personal friend of every great literary figure of his period.

"The house itself was built by Sir Edward Lutchins about

83

1932, but it stood on the site of the original Gogarty house, which was burnt down in the Troubled Times, some say without any reference to critical facts."

What Mr. Dillon meant was that the I.R.A. really had no business burning down this particular mansion. More great houses were destroyed by the Irish rebels for reasons hardly worthy of arson than in ten centuries of warfare. Ownership by a Britisher, or alleged ownership by an absentee landlord, was enough for the partisans to destroy the property. It reminded me of the Thirty Years' War in Europe when mere adherence to the Catholic or Protestant faith by the owner was enough to have the house destroyed by the opposition.

"What happened after the fire?" I asked.

"The site being one of the most beautiful in Ireland, between the lake and the sea, the hotel was then built. This was in 1922. Following the rebuilding of the house, Gogarty, who ran it as a rather literary type of hotel, collected there a number of interesting people, among them the poet and Nobel prize winner W. B. Yeats, whose centenary we are celebrating this year. And Yeats, of course, was very interested in psychic phenomena of one kind or another and has written a number of plays and stories on the subject. He also went in for séances. We were told that some of the séances held at Renvyle were very successful.

"Now the background to the piece of information which I have is that during the years preceding my arrival it had been noted that one particular room in this hotel was causing quite a bit of bother. On one or two occasions people came down saying there was *somebody* in the room, and on one very particular occasion, a lady whom I knew as a sane and sensible person complained that a man was looking over her shoulder while she was making her face up at the mirror. This certainly caused some furor."

"I can imagine—watching a lady put on her 'face' is certainly an invasion of privacy—even for a ghost," I observed.

"Well," Mr. Dillon continued, "when I went there the hotel had been empty for about a year and a half. It had been taken over by a new company and I opened it for that new company. My wife and I found some very unpleasant sensations while we were there."

"What did you do?"

"Finally, we got the local parish priest to come up and do something about it."

"Did it help?"

"The entire house had this atmosphere about it. We had Mass said in the place, during which there was a violent thunderstorm. We somehow felt that the situation was under control. About August of that particular year, my wife was ill and my father was staying in the hotel at the time. I moved to that particular room where the trouble had been. It is located in the center of the building facing into a courtyard. The house is actually built on three sides of a courtyard. It is one flight up. This was thirteen years ago now, in August of 1952."

"What happened to you in the haunted room, Mr. Dillon?" I asked.

"I went to sleep in this room," he replied, "and my father decided he would sleep in the room also. He is a particularly heavy sleeper, so nothing bothers him. But I was rather tired and I had worked terribly hard that day, and as I lay in bed I suddenly heard this loud, clicking noise going on right beside my ears as if someone wanted to get me up! I refused to go—I was too tired—so I said, 'Will you please go away, whoever you are?'—and I put my blanket over my head and went to sleep."

"What do you make of it?" I said.

"There is a strong tradition that this room is the very room in which Yeats carried out these séances, and for that reason there was left there as a legacy actually some being of some kind which is certainly not explainable by ordinary standards."

"Has anyone else had experiences there?"

"Not the finger clicking. I assume that was to get my attention. But the wife of a musician here in town, whom I know well, Molly Flynn—her husband is Eamon O'Gallcobhair, a well-known Irish musician—had the experience with the man looking over her shoulder. He was tall and dressed in dark clothes."

"Have more people slept in this room and had experiences?"

"Over the years, according to the staff, about ten different people have had this experience. None of them knew the reputation the house had as being haunted, incidentally."

The reports of an intruder dated back only to Yeats' presence in the house, but of course something might have been latently present, perhaps "held over" from the earlier structure, and merely awakened by the séances.

It was not until the following summer that our hopes to go to Renvyle House were realized. Originally we had asked our friend Dillon to get us rooms at this renowned resort hotel so we could combine research with a little loafing in the sun—but as fate would have it, by the time we were ready to name a date for our descent upon the Emerald Isle, every nook and cranny at Renvyle House had been taken. Moreover, we could not even blame our ever present countrymen, for the American tourist, I am told, waits far too long to make his reservations. The Britisher, on the other hand, having been taught caution and prevision by a succession of unreliable governments, likes to "book rooms," as they say, early in the season, and consequently we found that Connemara was once again British—for the summer, anyway.

We were given the choice of bedding down at nearby Leenane where Lord ffrench is the manager of a rather modern hotel built directly upon the rocky Connemara soil on the shore of a lough several miles deep. These loughs, or fjords, as they are called in Norway, are remnants of the ice ages, and not recommended for swimming, but excellent for fishing, since the Connemara fish apparently don't mind the cold.

I should explain at this point that Connemara is the name of an ancient kingdom in the westernmost part of Ireland, which was last—and least—in accepting English custom and language, and so it is here in the cottages along the loughs and the magnificent Connemara seacoast that you can hear the softly melodic tongue of old Erin still spoken as a natural means of expression. This, of course, is a far cry from the politically inspired "Gaelization" of Irish public life, which is not likely to succeed since Gaelic is impractical for modern business relations, no matter how pretty it sounds. Any language that spells Owen "Eoin," O'Gonahue "O'Gallcobhair," and Dunleary "Dun Laoghaire," is not likely to be practical. But the Irish need not worry about speaking English, a foreign tongue: the way many of them speak it, you would never know it is the same language. The lilting brogue and the strange construction of sentences is as different from what you can hear across the Straits as day and night. There is, of course, a small percentage of literary and upper-class Irishmen, especially in Dublin, whose English is so fine it outshines that spoken in Albion, and that, too, is a kind of moral victory over the English. Just as the citizens of Prague, Bohemia, know that their German is better than that spoken anywhere in Germany.

But we have left Lord ffrench waiting for our arrival at the Hotel Leenane, and await us he did, a charming, middle-thirtyish man wild about fishing and genially aware of the lure the area has for tourists. Leenane was pleasant and the air was fresh and clear, around 65 degrees at a time when New York was having a comfortable 98 in the shade. My only complaint about the hotel concerned the walls, which had the thickness of wallpaper.

The weather this month of July, 1966, was exceptionally fine and had been so for weeks, with a strong sun shining down on our heads as we set out for Renvyle after lunch. The manager, Paul Hughes, had offered to come and fetch us in his car, and he—the manager, not the car—turned out to be far younger than I had thought. At 27, he was running a major hotel and running it well. It took us about three-quarters of an hour, over winding roads cut through the ever present Connemara rock, to reach the coastal area where Renvyle House stands on a spot just about as close to America—except for the Atlantic—as any land could be in the area. The sea was fondling the very shores of the land on which the white two-story house stood, and cows and donkeys were everywhere around it, giving the entire scene a bucolic touch. Mr. Hughes left us alone for a while to take the sun in the almost tropical garden. After lunch I managed to corner him in the bar. The conversation, in Sybil Leek's presence, had avoided all references to ghosts, of course. But now Sybil was outside, looking over the souvenir shop, and Hughes and I could get down to the heart of the matter.

Mr. Hughes explained that the hotel had been rebuilt in 1930 over an older house originally owned by the Blakes, one of the Galway tribes, who eventually sold it to Oliver St. John Gogarty. I nodded politely, as Mr. Dillon had already traced the history of the house for me last summer.

"He was a doctor in Dublin," Hughes explained, "and he came here weekends and entertained people such as Joyce and Yeats and Augustus John."

Thank goodness, I thought, they did not have autograph hounds in Connemara!

Mr. Hughes had been the manager for three years, he explained.

"Ever notice anything unusual about any of the rooms?" I prodded.

"No, I haven't, although many of the staff have reported strange happenings. It seems that one of the maids, Rose Coine, saw a man in one of the corridors upstairs—a man who disappeared into thin air."

Miss Coine, it developed, was middle-aged, and rather shy. This was her week off, and though we tried to coax her later, at her own cottage, to talk about her experiences, she refused.

"She has experienced it a few times," Mr. Hughes continued. "I don't know how many, though."

"Has anyone else had unusual impressions anywhere in the hotel?"

"They say since the hotel was rebuilt it isn't as strong anymore."

"But didn't Miss Coine have her experience *after* the fire?"

"Yes," the manager admitted, "last year."

I decided to pay the haunted room, number 27, a visit. This was the room mentioned by Eoin Dillon in which he had encountered the ghostly manifestations. We ascended the wooden staircase, with Sybil joining us—my wife and I, and Mr. Hughes, who had to make sure the guests of number 27 were outside for the moment. The room we entered on the second floor was a typical vacation-time hotel room, fairly modern and impersonal in decor, except for a red fireplace in the center of the left wall. I later learned that the two rooms now numbered 27 and 18 were originally one larger room. I took some photographs and let Sybil gather impressions. Hughes quickly closed the outside door to make sure nobody would disturb us. Sybil sat down in the chair before the fireplace. The windows gave onto the courtyard.

"I have the feeling of something overlapping in time," Sybil Leek began. Of course, she had no idea of the "two Renvyles" and the rebuilding of the earlier house.

"I have a peculiar feeling around my neck," she continued, "painful feeling, which has some connection with this particular room, for I did not feel it a moment ago downstairs."

"Do you feel a presence here?" I asked directly.

"Yes," Sybil replied at once, "something . . . connected with pain. I feel as if my neck's broken."

I took some more pictures; then I heard Sybil murmur "1928." I immediately questioned her about the significance of this date. She felt someone suffered in the room we were in at that time. Also, the size of the room has been changed since.

"There is a presence in this area," she finally said with resolution. "A noisy presence. This person is rough."

After Sybil remarked that it might be difficult to get the fireplace going, we went to the adjoining room to see if the impressions there might be stronger.

"What do you sense here?" I asked.

"Fear."

"Can it communicate?"

"It is not the usual thing we have . . . just pain, strong pain."

"Someone who expired here?"

"Yes, but did not finish completely."

"Is the person here now?"

"Not the person, but an impression."

"How far back?"

"I only get as far back as 1928."

I questioned Paul Hughes. That was indeed the time of the Yeats séances.

"What sort of people do you feel connected with this room?"

"There is this overlapping period . . . 1928 I feel very vital, but beyond that we go down in layers . . . travelling people, come here, do not live here . . . does the word 'off-lander' mean anything?"

It did not to me.

"We're in 1928 now. Men in long dresses . . . religious, perhaps . . . men in long clothes? A group of men, no women. Perhaps ten men. Long coats. Sitting in front of a big fire."

"The one you feel hung up in the atmosphere here—is he of the same period?"

"No," Sybil replied, "this is of a later period."

"How did he get here?"

"This is someone who was living here . . . died in this room . . . fire . . . the people in the long clothes are earlier, can't tell if they're men or women, could be monks, too . . . but the one whom I feel in the atmosphere of this room, he is from 1928."

We left the room and walked out into the corridor, the same corridor connecting the area in which we had just been with number 2, farther back in the hotel. It was here that the ghost had been observed by the maid, I later learned. Sybil mentioned that there were ten people with long clothes, but she could not get more.

"Only like a photograph," she insisted.

We proceeded to the lovely library, which is adorned with wooden panelling and two rather large paintings of Saints Brigid and Patrick—and I noticed that St. Brigid wore the long, robe-like dress of the ancient Gaelic women, a dress, incidentally, that some of Ireland's 19th century poets imitated for romantic reasons. It reminded Sybil of what she had felt in the room upstairs.

From her own knowledge, she recalled that William Butler Yeats had a lady friend fond of wearing such ancient attire! Far-fetched though this sounded, on recollection I am not so sure. We left the house, and Paul Hughes drove us up a mountain road to the cottage in which the maid who had seen the ghost lived.

Hughes would go in first and try and persuade her to talk to me. Should he fail, he would then get the story once more from her and retell it to us afresh. We waited about fifteen minutes in his car while the manager tried his native charm on the frightened servant woman. He emerged and shook his head. But he had at least succeeded in having her tell of her experiences to him once more.

"About a year ago," Hughes began, "in the ground floor corridor leading to room number 2, Mrs. Coine saw a man come through the glass door and go into room 2."

"What did she do?" I interrupted.

"It suddenly struck Miss Coine that there was nobody staying in room 2 at the time. So she went down into room 2 and could not see anybody! She suddenly felt weak, and the housekeeper was coming along wondering what had happened to her. But she would not talk about it at first for she thought it would be bad for business at the hotel."

"Ridiculous," I said. "American tourists adore ghosts."

"Well," Hughes continued, "earlier this year—1966—there was a lady staying in room 2. Her daughter was in room 38. After two nights, she insisted on leaving room 2 and was happy to take a far inferior room instead. There were no complaints after she had made this change."

I discovered that rooms 2 and 27 were in distant parts of the hotel, just about as far apart as they could be.

There was a moment of silence as we sat in the car and I thought it all over.

"Did she say what the man looked like that she saw?" I finally asked, referring to Miss Coine's ghost.

"Yes," Hughes replied and nodded serenely. "*A tall man*, a very tall man."

"And a flesh and blood man could not have left the room by other means?"

"Impossible. At that stage the new windows had not yet been put in and the windows were inoperable with the exception of a small fan window. This happened about lunchtime, after Mass, on Sunday. In 1965."

"And the strange behavior of the lady?"

"Between Easter and Whitsun, this year, 1966."

We walked back into the main lobby of the hotel. There, among other memorabilia, were the framed pictures of great Irish minds connected with Renvyle House.

Among them, of course, one of William Butler Yeats.

I looked at it, long and carefully. Yeats was *a tall man*, a very tall man. . . .

*   *   *

In the winter of 1952-1953, Oliver St. John Gogarty wrote a brief article for *Tomorrow* magazine, entitled "Yeats and the Ghost of Renvyle Castle."

To begin with, the term castle was applied by *Tomorrow*'s editors, since Gogarty knew better than to call Renvyle House a castle. There *is* a Renvyle castle all right and it still stands, about two miles south of the hotel, a charred ruin of medieval masonry, once the property of the celebrated Irish pirate queen Grania O'Malley.

Gogarty's report goes back to the house that stood there prior to the fire. Our visit was to the new house, built upon its ruins. The popular tale of séances held at the Renvyle House must refer to the earlier structure, as none were held in the present one, as far as I know.

Gogarty's report tells of Yeats and his own interest in the

occult; of one particular time when Mrs. Yeats, who was a medium, told of seeing a ghostly face at her window; of a séance held in an upstairs room in which the restless spirit of a young boy manifested who had died by his own hands there. Morgan Even, a Welshman who apparently was also a trance medium, was among the guests at the time, and he experienced an encounter with the ghost which left him frightened and weak.

"I felt a strange sensation. A feeling that I was all keyed up just like the tension in a nightmare, and with that terror that nightmares have. Presently, I saw a boy, stiffly upright, in brown velvet with some sort of shirt showing at his waist. He was about twelve. Behind the chair he stood, all white-faced, hardly touching the floor. It seemed that if he came nearer some awful calamity would happen to me. I was just as tensed up as he was—nightmare terrors, tingling air; but what made it awful was my being wide awake. The figure in the brown velvet only looked at me, but the atmosphere in the room vibrated. I don't know what else happened. I saw his large eyes, I saw the ruffles on his wrists. He stood vibrating. His luminous eyes reproved. He looked deeply into mine.

"The apparition lifted his hands to his neck and then, all of a sudden, his body was violently seized as if by invisible fiends and twisted into horrible contortions in mid-air. He was mad! I sympathized for a moment with his madness and felt myself at once in the electric tension of Hell. Suicide! Suicide! Oh, my God, he committed suicide in this very house."

As it transpired, the ghost had communicated with Yeats through automatic writing. He objected to the presence of strangers in his house. But Yeats responded to his objection with a list of commands of his own such as the ghost could hardly have expected. First, he must desist from frightening the children in their early sleep. He must cease to moan about the chimneys. He must walk the house no more. He must not move furniture or terrify those who sleep nearby. And, finally, he was ordered to name himself to Yeats. And this he did.

How could Yeats, a visitor, have known that the children

used at times to rush down crying from their bedroom? Nor could he have guessed that it was the custom of the Blake family to call their sons after the Heptarchy. And yet he found out the ghost's particular name. A name Gogarty had never gleaned from the local people though he lived for years among them.

The troubled spirit had promised to appear in the ghost room to Mrs. Yeats, as he was before he went mad sixty years before.

Presently, Mrs. Yeats appeared carrying a lighted candle. She extinguished it and nodded to her husband. "Yes, it is just as you said."

"My wife saw a pale-faced, red-haired boy of about fourteen years of age standing in the middle of the north room. She was by the fireplace when he first took shape. He had the solemn pallor of a tragedy beyond the endurance of a child. He resents the presence of strangers in the home of his ancestors. He is Harold Blake."

And now it became clear to me *what* Sybil Leek had felt! Upstairs, in the room nearly on the same spot where the ghostly boy had appeared in the *old* house, she had suddenly felt a terrible discomfort in her neck—just as the psychic Welshman had, all those years ago! Was she reliving the tragedy or was the pale boy still about?

But the maid had seen a tall stranger, not a young boy, and not in the haunted room, but far from it. Yeats had been terribly attached to this house, and, being a man of great inquisitiveness, was just the type to stay on even after death. If only to talk to the melancholy boy from his own side of the Veil!

Welcome Back to Ireland, or
Failte Fails Us

S O MANY UNFINISHED CASES WERE LEFT ON OUR HANDS IN 1965 that a return to Ireland seemed unavoidable—not that I felt I wanted to avoid going back to this wonderful land. I made one mistake, however. I picked the wrong time. Now there is nothing so wonderful as an Irish welcome, no one so genial as a Dublin host. Except during tourist season. That is when you can't get a hotel room in Dublin because the German spenders got there ahead of you, or the lady from Detroit or the London clerk.

"You have very little chance of having your requirements fulfilled in July or August," J. P. Murray of the *Bord Failte* or Tourist Board informed me candidly. "We would, of course, be pleased to mark your card (map) for you and give you whatever briefing you might require." Imagine that! And no charge for marking up my roadmap.

I was so overcome by this generous offer of assistance, I took up the matter of suitable accommodations with my American friend George Foley, who represents some Irish interests, and before you could say "Who needs the Tourist Board?" I had reservations at Jury's Hotel on College Green, Dublin. Jury's turned out to be a sprawling, modern hotel, overcrowded of course and a far cry from the Shelbourne of the season before, but in its own way pleasant and comfortable. I even managed to find a public-relations-conscious young man in the person of Gerard Enright who made our many press and radio interviews smoother.

The Dublin press pounced upon us immediately after our arrival on a very warm July Monday in 1966. I was in no mood for it, having just been informed that our luggage had been "mislaid" somewhere in Europe. We spent all day alternately phoning various airports and fending off reporters who did not bother to phone up for permission from downstairs. Finally, we were esconced in our rooms and the program could be arranged. As I went through the considerable stack of mail awaiting us at Jury's, I became at once aware of the fact that our arrival had indeed already been preceded by some controversy.

It all started with poor Sybil Leek getting robbed in her St. Louis hotel room during a speaking engagement for the St. Louis Theosophical Society during the month of June. The eager press agent for the society sent out a memorandum to the press, telling the world that Mrs. Leek was so enraged about her losses that she had cursed the thief and no good would befall him. This went around the world via United and Associated Press wires in various elaborate forms. The one that got into the Irish papers started with "Witch says all hell will break loose for thief" and went on to describe that said unfortunate man or woman would indeed suffer terribly, if the witch was right. It was a first-class piece of hack writing and I could laugh at it. Sybil of course never said anything like it to anyone. I called a press conference to set the matter straight, and most of the papers published factual accounts of our purpose in Ireland. They particularly liked Mrs. Leek's great-grandmother, who was an O'Brien, and our avowed purpose of looking for a home—non-haunted—in Ireland.

Then I got the shock of the year. In the mail was a letter from a lady who had invited us to her castle because it had a resident ghost. The castle in County Wexford looked as a good old haunted Irish castle should look, with ivy-overgrown towers and old trees all around it.

"On behalf of my brother, his wife and myself I would like to say how happy we should be to welcome you all to Huntington," the castle's owner had written me in New York. "There is an extra visitor we should particularly enjoy meeting. We hear that Mrs. Leek has a wonderful jackdaw. . . . Our spirit friends and ancestors here are very friendly, so you will be able to sleep nicely."

The writer evidently knew all about Sybil and her jackdaw, but then Sybil's publicity as a "White Witch" has been world-wide for years.

"We certainly look forward to the séance," the lady wrote me a little later, when I had settled on two days that we could manage to spend at their place, what with the pressure of so many invitations in Ireland.

But when the lady read the fantastic story about Sybil's burglary, complete with cursing the thief, things were a little different.

"My brother, sister-in-law and myself were very upset . . . this puts us into an embarrassing position. For while we have no prejudice against White Witchcraft, we cannot associate ourselves with the particular attitude publicized in this article. We therefore have to ask you to withdraw our invitation to Mrs. Leek to come here. . . . My sister-in-law is very much concerned that there should be no publicity about our home. . . . I should perhaps mention that my brother is an Anglican clergyman."

So, if this lady's castle is still haunted, she missed a good opportunity to find out!

The *Irish Times* story about Sybil's non-existent curse also burned the ears of a gentleman named Marcus Clement, who owns Lough Rynn castle at Mohill, in County Leitrim in the North of Ireland. My interest in this particular old house was sparked by a note from one Joseph Parkes of Athlone. It would seem that the castle was occupied by a Cavalry Squadron of the Eire Army during the last war and Mr. Parkes served in it as a NCO. Several of his men reported ghostly disturbances in the castle in the early morning hours while on sentry duty. Mr. Clement had invited us to come and see for ourselves if there were any ghosts left. He was more interested in archaeology since his demesne also included some very early ruins.

Mr. Clement wrote that his uncle who was perhaps "psychic" had excavated an oratory. The existence of this oratory was unknown until 1902 when the poet AE (George Russell) had an experience there which led Mr. Clement's uncle to have some digging done and the ruins were uncovered. Mr. Clement added that he did not know of any authentic psychic occurrences connected with this house though there were the usual kind of rumors.

I never got the chance to find out if any of those "usual kind of rumors" were true.

On July 14 I received an urgent message from both Mr. and Mrs. Clement—separately, to make sure I got it—asking me not to come. It was the first time in my long career as Ghost Hunter that anyone had asked me *not* to come. Usually, they beg to please come and it is I who have to say no because of too many other cases already requiring my attention. If anything, it has proved to me that prejudice and superstition can be very pronounced in Ireland.

Mrs. Clement blamed her sudden lack of hospitality on the servant problem. The country people in Leitrim, she said, are very superstitious and nervous, and they had had a lot of trouble keeping staff in their house. (Aha! I thought, ghosts or merely low wages?) She felt that my visit would continue their servants in their suspicions.

Mr. Clement, despite his scientific approach and self-proclaimed skepticism in occult matters, further took umbrage at the fabricated stories about Sybil's alleged curse. He claimed that a study of the press in Ireland and abroad had revealed that my associate Miss Leak [*sic*] was a practitioner of the black arts. The report in the *Irish Times* of her recent activities in the United States of America had not recommended her as the sort of person Mr. Clement would like to have about.

By now I was convinced that Sybil had committed a terrible faux pas by getting herself robbed and slugged.

Fortunately, these were the only exceptions to the many friendly invitations we received from young and old. Two 13-year-old girls going to school at the Convent of the Child Jesus in nearby Killiney wrote us, offering to help our research by house-to-house canvassing for ghosts.

"I annoy all our guests intensively by asking them if they have seen ghosts and I have discovered about sixty per cent of them have," one of the girls, Clodagh Simonds, wrote. I thanked them for their enthusiasm and cautioned them about *guests* as well as *ghosts.* . . .

A long-standing invitation to Powerscourt, one of Ireland's most magnificent houses, was finally honored when industrialist Ralph Slazenger picked us up in his little car. Within half an hour we had left bustling Dublin and found ourselves in the country, far from traffic noises or crowds.

Powerscourt with its French gardens is a showplace and its many rooms are frequently used for social doings, charity events, and the like. Tourists may see part of the house for a small fee. The Slazengers—Mr. and Mrs. and five grown children—live in it in the manner of upper middle class business people, very efficiently and happily. Mrs. Slazenger runs the farming part of it. Slazenger himself is rather well read on psychic subjects, I soon discovered.

Was there a ghost in the house? Michael, one of the sons, insisted there was a passage that gave him the creeps and we dutifully had a look at it. But neither Sybil nor Catherine felt anything specially spooky at the spot, so the ghost, if there was one, must have moved out along with the Viscount Powerscourts when they sold the house!

Not far from Dublin is another magnificent country palace belonging to a lady well known in international society. I asked permission for a visit, which the lady granted, and I was disappointed only by her reluctance to let me use her name. For she is a highly sensitive person, mediumistic herself, who has had more than her share of brushes with the uncanny. The place boasts some hundred rooms which she has mostly decorated herself in exquisite taste; it does not have the formal gardens of Powerscourt, but it has a sundial set amid meadowland and a view into the distance that equals that showplace's surroundings in attractiveness. It was here that a reporter from the *Irish Independent* by the name of James Brennan experienced an apparition of a ghost, and the house was the seat of a family associated with certain immoral practices in the 17th and 18th centuries. One of the owners took the wrong side in the Civil Wars of the 18th century and was barbarously executed by the townspeople for it. It is *his* ghost, allegedly, that still walks the corridors of the older portions of the house.

That there is still another phantom in this place is certain. Sybil, walking along the many passages, suddenly came to a full stop in what turned out to be the oldest part of the house. She felt a female ghost there.

"This point has been the scene of some violence," Sybil said. "There is a sickly feeling about it that is nowhere else in the house. Emotional conflict, particularly nasty in nature."

"More than one ghost?" I asked. It was such a big house.

We went upstairs, into the large bedroom in which most of the reported phenomena had occurred.

"I want to sink down," Sybil said quickly. "I know I am upstairs, but somehow I feel I must go down. Instead of green, I see only gray walls. They are not really there, but for me they are. A male and a female presence here."

"What can you tell me about them?"

"The male has the emotional conflict, I think . . . I wonder if he could have run away? Someone leaving very quickly . . . not dying, just leaving . . . a constant coming and going . . . one man comes and goes constantly, over a long period of time . . . always leaving emotional conflict behind him . . . the male predominates, but it is the female personality who is so sickening to me . . . she is the disturbed one. . . ."

"Are they of the same period?"

"No," Sybil replied, "the female presence is the older presence. The male is later and there is quite a gap between them."

Later, the lady of the house confirmed that she herself, as well as others, had seen a wraith in that part of the house—a woman in a long dress, evidently belonging to a much earlier period. Her own interest in the psychic had always been keen, and she knew that she was living with a couple of ghosts. Thus it was only natural that she wanted to find out who they were or what they wanted.

During one of many planchette sessions, the alleged ghost of the woman made contact with her and gave a name the lady had never heard of. Some time later she met a member of the family that owned the house in the earliest period. Accidentally, the name of an ancestor was mentioned. It was the same name obtained through the planchette!

One of the cases I came to Dublin to investigate concerned the *haunted fireplace* of Dunsandle. It all started with a short piece in *Fate* magazine many years ago under the title "The Haunted Mantelpiece." A report of a travelling ghost struck me as being, at the very least, unusual, for ghosts, as far as I knew, *stay put*. Here is what *Fate* had published:

"A weird account of a ghost that went with a mantelpiece recently was published in the Irish edition of the *Empire News*. The mantelpiece originally stood in Dunsandle Castle in Loughrey, County Galway, Ireland. It was purchased by Christy O'Neill, a marble sculptor of Dublin, who had it moved into his workshop.

"O'Neill said he was working late one evening when he happened to glance toward the mantelpiece and saw the shadowy figure of a tall man standing beside it. He walked forward for a closer look at the figure and was startled when it vanished. After that, O'Neill said, pieces of marble were thrown around the workshop, and his wife and grown-up children heard mysterious footsteps and strains of music.

"Deciding to get to the bottom of these strange happenings, O'Neill returned to Dunsandle Castle. He learned that the shadowy figure he described had been seen in the castle several times over the years. It had not, however, been seen since

O'Neill's purchase of the mantelpiece, which had stood in the quarters of a dead gamekeeper of one of the four barons of Dunsandle.

"O'Neill, it is reported, returned home, broke up the mantelpiece and threw the pieces on a scrap heap."

I questioned the last paragraph, for a sensible Irish sculptor is not likely to throw away a good fireplace.

On November 16, 1965, a gentleman named Roger Kilbride got in touch with me.

"In the latter half of 1940 I was one of a party of thirty troops who were sent out from Renmore Barracks, Galway, to Dunsandle House, Athenry, as an advance party for the battalion. I was cook sergeant on that party and I and my staff were sleeping in the dining room which was converted into a temporary billet. On our third night there we were retired to bed at about 11:00 and were sitting up smoking and swapping yarns until midnight when we put out the lights. At approximately fifteen minutes after midnight we all heard a violin playing. The general opinion was that it was high class classical music and we said Carmody is gone in for highbrow stuff. Now Carmody, one of our party, was billeted in another part of the house and he was the only one of our party who played the violin. He gave recitals of Irish Airs from Radio Eireann. The following morning I reminded Carmody that in the future he do no fiddling after midnight but he informed me he had pawned his fiddle before leaving Renmore barracks. I then assumed it was music from the wireless in the officers' mess but Lt. Keohane assured me that the mess room was closed and he had retired at 11:00; he was the only officer with the party. I forgot about the incident after that and didn't hear any more music. Then on the 3rd November 1957 a new Sunday paper was launched, *The Sunday Review*, and I was a wholesale newsagent for same paper. Among its articles was this one. I came across: 'The Haunted Fireplace.' It appears after the troops left Dunsandle House in 1945 it was taken over by its original owner, Capt. Bowes Daly. Among some articles he sold was the fireplace in the room where I heard the music; this fireplace was purchased by a dealer in Dublin who installed it in his sitting room but had to have it removed on account of the strange violin music that came from it. I don't know what became of it after that."

Well, evidently the fireplace somehow got back to Dunsandle or there were two of them. I contacted the present owner of the old castle, Captain Bowes Daly, who brought me up to date on the status of castle and fireplace.

"I fear Dunsandle is now a ruin and I am now living at Cloghan Castle, Banagher, Offaly, the oldest inhabited castle in Ireland, built by my family in A.D. 1140. I have the fireplace installed here, but thank goodness, no ghosts!"

So the next time you hear violin music coming out of a fireplace let me know. Could be the ghost is fiddling while the fireplace burns!

Who Is the Ghost
at Number 118 Summerhill?

S UMMERHILL IS A MODEST STREET IN WHAT IS USUALLY RE-
ferred to as the Georgian section of old Dublin. Many of
the streets in this area have been demolished, and ugly modern
houses have taken the place of the old buildings. Thus it was no
surprise but rather a foregone conclusion that Summerhill Street
would also have to yield to pickaxe and shovel. When we visited
the area in July of 1966, a large gaping hole existed already in
the central portion of this once beautiful street, a hole where a
cluster of buildings once stood. But now it was nothing more
than a demolition site, an empty lot surrounded by the scarred
walls of old houses that, presumably, would fall next. Perhaps
one should not weep too loudly for the old houses, for it is also
true that many of them had over the years fallen into disrepair
and the people who have lived in them of late are of a much
lower class than those who originally built them.

My acquaintance with Summerhill dates to January 18, 1966,
when my good friend Patrick Byrne of the *Dublin Herald*
pointed out that there was a ghost doing all sorts of eerie things
in that street. At that time, the house numbered 118 was in the
process of being torn down.

The same day I received a clipping and note from Lord Dunalley, who had heard of my interest in psychic research. Lord Dunalley himself had had psychic experiences and his father had devoted a chapter in a book to ghosts, so we were on common ground. The first report, in recent times that is, of ghostly shenanigans on that spot came as a front-page surprise to shocked Dubliners who thought ghosts were akin to leprechauns, fairies and other charming but somewhat unreal manifestations of the Irish spirit.

The *Evening Press* reporter wrote on January 14, 1966:

"Six Dublin men are being terrified by strange happenings in a house at Summerhill. The men moved into the house, No. 118, just a week ago to demolish it, and since then work has been held up by a succession of strange events.

"Three of the men claim to have seen a ghost standing in one of the rooms, but on three different occasions. All three say they saw the strange figure clearly.

"The oldest member of the group, Mr. William McGregor, fainted and had to be revived.

"Now the men refuse to work on different floors in the house —they will not work at all unless they are allowed to remain on the same floor, within sight of each other.

" 'I saw the figure clearly,' said William McGregor, a partner in the firm which is carrying out the demolition work. 'He was a tall man, and seemed to be wearing a striped shirt, or overall, without a collar. The figure just stood there looking at me. I blessed myself and then I must have passed out.'

"Working with Mr. McGregor are his partner and foreman, Thomas Kearney, two sons, Christopher and William McGregor, and two workmen, Joseph Byrne and Noel Power.

"Said Joseph Byrne: 'I was wrestling with an old stove in the basement when I had a feeling someone was standing behind me. I looked around and saw nothing. After a while the same feeling crept over me and I had another look around.

" 'I saw a man, dressed in what appeared to be a butcher's striped jacket, standing looking towards a window. I shouted to the others, who were all working above me, but when they came down they couldn't see it at all.'

"The third man to see the strangely dressed figure was Mr. Kearney himself.

" 'I saw the man myself,' he told me. 'He wore the striped jacket or maybe it was a shirt but he had a napkin or something around his neck, and I was sure he looked like somebody who was dressed for a haircut or a shave.'

"The 'ghost of Summerhill' has hit the workmen like a bomb-shell. The demolition work has slowed up considerably because the men will not enter the three-storey house until it is bright and they leave it again as soon as the light begins to fade in the afternoon.

"None of them could be persuaded to take us down to the basement to see a large mural there, nor indeed would any of them venture upstairs again unless they all went in a group.

" 'There is something wrong with this house and it's playing badly on our nerves,' said Mr. McGregor, Senior. 'To tell you the truth, if it wasn't for the contract, I wouldn't work here another five minutes. A garda [policeman] told us yesterday that there had been reports of ghosts seen in the house before.' "

Other papers raced to interview the witnesses, but nothing materially new was unearthed. Dublin has its share of juvenile delinquents, and the following night they massed in force at the demolition site, carrying a large cross and shouting for the ghost to come out. It was all in the spirit of good, unclean fun.

A couple of days later, the Dublin reporter returned to the spot of the haunting. Things had come to a complete halt at the building site.

"Today demolition work was at a standstill in Summerhill's haunted house. No workmen turned up, and the only person there—apart from the ghost in the striped apron—was Christopher McGregor, one of the contractors.

"From the doorway, he surveyed the little groups of people

who had come to have a look (from a safe distance) and said: 'We have ten days to finish this job but it looks bad for today and we got little work done yesterday on account of the crowds who wanted to see the ghost.' "

These crowds included an American who had read this paper's story and wanted a conducted tour. He got it.

Mr. McGregor said: "The fellow swore he saw a shadow moving across that room up there. . . . I followed his pointed finger and saw only the skeleton of a room without floor or ceiling . . . and he offered to buy us out on the spot." No sale was made.

That number 118 Summerhill is really haunted was not a matter for doubt in the mind of any of the area's residents.

In his grocer's shop at 35 Stoneybatter, Mr. William Lynch told me the story of the ghost he knew of during the years he lived opposite the haunted house, from 1904 to 1950.

"There were three houses owned by the old, wealthy Hutton family who were the last of the city's coachbuilders. I recall as a child seeing carriages drive up for big parties.

"But it was 117 which was haunted then. Crowds used to gather and wait for the ghost to appear at midnight. I never saw it myself but I do know that in those days there were people who'd cross to the other side of the road passing 117.

"The ghost was supposed to have been seen at various times at the windows. The place had the look of a haunted house. It wasn't occupied, and the windows were barred and dust covered.

"In 1923 the Hutton family sold out to the then Dublin United Tramways Company, and the houses were converted into flats, later deteriorating into tenements. But the ghost stayed on. He moved into 118 when his haunt in 117 was pulled down."

I don't know about that American wanting "to buy them out," but what Mr. Lynch had to say was interesting. The *Evening Press* "stayed with the story" and a few days later again, on January 25, it published a couple of letters from residents of the area. One of them was from a gentleman signing himself Reamonn O'Corcorain, and he evidently knew his area well.

"I must confess I found the reports about the ghost in 118 Summerhill, Dublin, very interesting. I was born in Summerhill, and have lived all of my 20 years there.

"The present Summerhill C.I.E. bus garage and the houses—better known as the tramway houses—of which 118 is the last, were once the property of Thomas Hutton, the head of the celebrated firm of coachbuilders.

"A wealthy man with liberal sympathies, he married a highly accomplished woman from the Co. Down, whose interests ranged over a wide field—philosophy, art, politics.

"The youngest and favorite of the Hutton daughters was Annie who combined sweetness with distinction. It was at a dinner in Hutton's on December 22, 1843, Thomas Davis first met her. Thomas Hutton was already a subscriber to *The Nation*, the newspaper of the Young Ireland movement. The lane beside the garage is still known as Hutton's Lane."

Since I was unable to come to Dublin immediately, I asked Lord Dunalley to look into the case for me and to try and check out personally some of the material.

On February 1, 1966, I received his brief report.

"I visited the house again and spoke to the elderly man whose picture appeared on the page I sent you previously. I have little doubt that he saw the ghost. He is a simple man, a small demolition contractor, and admitted that he was so terrified that he fainted and had to be carried down by his mates from the top floor and revived. He told me that this ghost is said to be a Patrick Conway, a butcher who cut his throat in this house in 1863 and that this can be verified from the Dublin City Archives. Apart from these incidents during demolition there were previous complaints to the police about the haunting."

We came to Dublin on July 18 of the same year but it was not until the last day of our stay, the 23rd, that I found time to go to Summerhill with Sybil. I had left all the material about the case in New York, and thus was not too familiar with what I had read back in January and February. Sybil, of course, had no idea about the case. I made arrangements for a lady from the *Irish Times*, Irene ffrench, to take us to the site, since she had been kind to us in a piece in her paper. I also permitted a radio reporter named Neeson to join us there to record the experiment for both radio and television. I did not know of course what it would be like, whether Sybil would still get anything tangible from the demolished site—for house number 118 stood no more.

We arrived at the spot around four in the afternoon during one of those typically Irish on-again, off-again rainy periods, and Catherine did not exactly relish the idea of getting her hair wet. But bravely she trailed along with me carrying the tape recorder while I followed Sybil like a hunter following a bloodhound. Sybil made straight for the northwest corner of the lot.

"It's not very strong, you know," she mumbled, searching for clues.

"It is male," she added after a while.

"What period?" I asked.

"I don't feel a residence here . . . *something other than a house*. This male presence belongs to the previous period, before there was a residence here. I see green ground here."

"How far back?"

"1613 . . . I have this feeling of people passing through . . . ."

In retrospect, I find that the coach house—a station, not a residence—and "people passing through" would certainly match. Sybil, I repeat, never saw the newspaper accounts of the case.

"One man dominates . . . I would think that there was a way out here through the back wall . . . the land would be in that direction."

She was right; we were facing away from the center of Dublin towards what must have once been open country on the approaches to the city proper.

"I get the feeling of infiltration of overlapping periods," Sybil continued, "disturbances as late as 1932, but not very strong . . . there is violence here and blood-letting . . . the presence here, the people he came to meet did not arrive . . . something went wrong at this last meeting point. . . ."

"Do you think that by tearing down the house we have disposed of the ghost?"

Sybil shook her head.

"No, they will have to go beyond this foundation . . . several occasions of violence . . . ."

I told Sybil then that people had experienced phenomena in the area, without, however, giving any details or names.

When she heard that someone tearing down the building had made contact with the ghost she pointed out that that might have aroused the spectre to anger, for the building was his own home.

"He needs to communicate . . . he is stranded, waiting for someone."

Sybil thought this was the 17th century gentleman she felt in the spot.

No butcher in a striped shirt. But so it is with mediums sometimes; they get one layer but not another. Especially when the house is completely gone. Quite possibly when the house at number 118 came tumbling down, the ghostly butcher went with it and gave the 17th century ghost a chance to be felt by our friend. We will have to wait for a new building to rise on the site to determine whether the butcher or the gentleman who had to wait will move back in . . . or whether it will be, in addition to being dust-proof, also *ghost-proof!*

BALINGULLE
DUBLIN

C. Buchanan
8-66

The Secret of Ballinguile

"YOU MAY LIKE TO FOLLOW UP THE ENCLOSED," WROTE
Patrick Byrne of the *Dublin Herald*, who had been running pieces about our impending return to Ireland in search of
haunted houses. The enclosure turned out to be a letter written
in longhand, dated April 2nd, 1966, from a Mrs. O'Ferrall, who
had a sister living near Dartry, a suburb of Dublin, said sister
having but recently removed there from a haunted house on
Eglington Road, Donnybrook.

After a consultation about the matter—talking about ghosts
is not taken lightly by the Irish—Mrs. O'Ferrall got her sister's
approval, and, more important, address. Thus it was that I
addressed myself to Mrs. Mary Healy of Temple Road, so that
I might learn of her adventures in the house first hand.

The house in question, it turned out, was still standing, but
had lately been falling into disrepair, since the new owners were
bent on eventual demolition. Mrs. Healy had sold it in 1963.
Part of the sprawling gray stone house is 18th century and part
is 19th, but the site has been inhabited continuously since at
least the 15th century. A high wall that surrounds the property
gives it the appearance of a country house rather than a city
residence, which it is, for Donnybrook is really a part of Dublin.

The word Donnybrook, incidentally, is derived from St. Broc, a local patron, and there is on the grounds of this house, called *Ballinguile*, a natural well of great antiquity, dedicated to St. Broc.

Thus it is that the house may have given the whole district its name. The well, situated towards the rear wall of the garden, is greatly overgrown with lush vegetation, for everything grows well in moist Ireland. The house itself is set back a bit from the road—a busy road it is—thus affording a degree of privacy. In back of the main house are a now totally rundown flower and vegetable garden, and the extensive stables, long fallen into disuse or partially used as garages. There is farther back a small, compact gatehouse, still occupied by a tenant who also vaguely looks after the empty house itself.

There are large sitting rooms downstairs fore and aft, attesting to the somewhat haphazard fashion in which the house was altered and added to over the years. The house consists of three portions, with the middle portion the highest; there is a second story, and above it an attic to which one gains access only by a metal ladder. Set down in front of the sidewall of Ballinguile is a greenhouse which a previous owner had made into a kind of verandah. Now it lay in shambles, just as most of the ground-floor windows had long been shattered by neighborhood youngsters in a peculiar spirit of defiance common to all young people wherever unbroken—and unattended—windows stare!

"The principal unusual happenings," Mrs. Healy explained, "were the sound of footsteps, mostly on the stairs. They were so natural that one did not at once realize that all the household were present. They occurred during the daytime and most frequently during July and August. In fact, August was the time the two strangest things happened. The year I moved there, my youngest son was living with me and he was still a student and a bit lively. When he had friends in I usually retired and went to bed.

"One night he had just one friend downstairs, and about 9 p. m. came to me and said they were going out for a while, and so they went. Shortly after I woke from a doze to hear a lot of people downstairs; they were laughing and joking, and talking, and I could hear them moving about. They seemed very happy and really enjoying themselves. I was very angry and thought to get up and tell them that was no time to be having an unprepared party, but I didn't.

"After quite a while there was silence, and shortly after, the hall door opened and my son came in. He had gone to see his friend home and stayed with him a while. *There had been no party!*

"Two years later, also in August, my daughter, who lived with her husband and little girl in half the house, and I were standing in my dining room, an old converted kitchen. Suddenly we saw the little girl of three and a half talking to someone in the enclosed yard. She would say something and wait for the answer. There was no one that we could see anywhere, but we distinctly heard her say, 'but you are my friend!' We asked her who she was speaking to and she said casually, 'the tall dark man,' and gave us the impression she knew him well.

"Just before we left, one evening after we had all retired to bed about 11 p. m., we were aroused by the door bell. My son-in-law went down to find two policemen inquiring if all was well. Passing, they had heard a lot of violent noise in the house, and seeing all dark, came to investigate.

"We had heard nothing!

"To me the strangest thing was that one did not feel frightened, everything seemed so completely natural. It was only afterwards one realized it was strange. At no time was there any 'creepy' feeling.

"The only person who was frightened at night was the little girl, who would not stay in bed at night saying something frightened her. But children often do that. We did not tell her anything about our own experiences, for children are quick to elaborate."

So much for Mrs. Healy's experiences. I reported none of this to Sybil, of course, and as we were on the lookout for a house to buy in Ireland, it was simply still another house to inspect for that reason.

On arrival in Dublin I arranged a date to meet Mrs. Healy at her new home, after we had been to the former Healy home in Donnybrook. To get permission and keys, I telephoned the present owner, Arthur Lurie, who was most cooperative although I never told him about any potential ghost. But then I doubt it would have impressed him. Mr. Lurie sounded to me like a man who was all business. The price he asked for the house was unfortunately too high for us, but we did like the house and might have bought it otherwise.

Keys in pocket, we set out for Ballinguile on a very warm July afternoon. The driver obligingly opened the rusty gates for us and the car drove into the grounds. At that moment, a little lady practically flew past us in pursuit of two small dogs, explaining on the run— "They used to play in here, you know. Mind if I give them a run?"

Before we could answer she was past us and inside. Five minutes later I had her out again, dogs and all.

Now we started our exploration, carefully avoiding the many broken windows that had let in a veritable avalanche of birds, to whom some rooms had become home, judging from their evidences.

We were still standing outside, while the driver was napping in the sun. I was busy putting my tape recording equipment and cameras into operating condition, while Catherine explored the wider reaches of the lush garden. Sybil and I found ourselves directly outside the rear sitting room.

Suddenly, *I heard muffled voices* coming from the room and my first thought was, oh, there are some other people here also; how inconsiderate of the landlord to send them at the same time! Sybil turned her head to me and there was one big question mark written all over her face. She, too had heard the voices. It was over in a matter of perhaps two or three seconds, and the voices, one of which was male and deep, sounded as if coming from under water, but they certainly were human voices in conversation . . . *such as at a party!* We entered the room immediately, but of course there wasn't a soul in it.

I decided it was time to enter the house and see what Sybil's psychic sense would "get" us.

"Funny thing," Sybil remarked as we started up the path towards the house, "I feel as if I'd been here before. I've 'seen' this house many times over the years. This house had a lot of unwarranted hatred directed towards it. When we got out of the car, I thought I saw a man . . . in one of the upper rooms . . . I thought I heard a voice . . . something beginning with S, like Sure, or Sean . . . the central portion, upper window, there seemed to be a man reading a paper . . . ."

Since Sybil did not get any strong impressions in the downstairs part of the house, we ascended the stairs and soon found ourselves on the second floor, in the very room in which most of the psychic occurrences had taken place.

"There is plotting here . . . in this particular room I have the feeling of somebody very sick, worried, very excitable, a man —not too far back, the grounds seem to have an older influence but not this room. About 300 years on the grounds, but in the house, perhaps fifty years. There is a foreign influence here. Another language."

"Can you get any names?" I asked as Sybil leaned against the wall of the empty room. There was no chair to sit down in, so we had to do our trance work in this awkward fashion.

"Wyman," Sybil mumbled now, and gradually she became more and more entranced, although at no time was she in full trance.

"French influence . . . Wyban, Vyvern . . . don't know what it means," she added, "he is here now. Not too long ago. He's the one who brought us here."

"What does he want us to do?"

I too had felt that this case was more than routine, that we were drawn to this house in some mysterious way. *What was the secret of Ballinguile?*

"It seems ridiculous, but the man looks like Abraham Lincoln,"

Sybil finally stated, "thin, gaunt, stooping shoulders . . . it's his house, fifty years ago . . . Whibern . . . he has papers . . . something to be careful about . . . the land . . . the deed, there is trouble . . . the house and the land are not completely together."

I discovered later that the house was built on ground that belonged to different owners and that there were great legal problems involved in this. Sybil had no knowledge of this fact.

"Another man knows this," Sybil continued. "There is some trouble about the land. That's the conflict of two families. He wants us to settle the land. Samly, Seamly . . . that was the name that was spelled when I came into the house. It's a family name."

"Did he die here?"

There was a moment of silence as Sybil queried the ghost.

"Reading the papers carefully," she finally mumbled instead, "check the papers, Miss Seamly . . . check the papers carefully . . . the money was wrong . . . Simmely (Seamly) made a mistake about the ground . . . sort it out . . ."

Sybil was almost in trance now and her voice became weak and irregular. "Twenty-four," she whispered under the influence of the ghost, "1924 . . . year . . . ."

"Is there any other problem?" I inquired matter-of-factly. Might as well clean out the lot.

"The woman," Sybil said, "where did she go? He says the woman left!"

I assured him there was nobody here now but us ghost hunters. Did he want us to buy the house perhaps? Not that it would help with the landlord.

"Good people," he mumbled, "people from overseas live here . . . now . . . not for the Irish . . . traitors . . . stolen the land . . . the land to the Institute . . . Institute for sick people . . . ."

"Did you leave the land to the Institute?" I asked.

"Took it . . . the Institute. . . ."

"And who should have gotten it instead?"

"Wyman . . . Wynan." The name still was not quite clear, but I promised we would try and look into the matter of the land if we could.

"He knows . . ." Sybil murmured, and a moment or two later she came out of the state bordering on trance. We were still upstairs.

Sybil remembered absolutely nothing, but "her eyes did not feel right" for a moment.

We went downstairs and closed the house, got into the car and drove to the nearby house where Mrs. Healy and her married daughter now reside.

Suddenly it struck me that Sybil had talked about a man named White ever since we had met again in Dublin. Did I know any Mr. White? I did not. Would we be meeting such a person in one of our investigations? No, I said, we would not as far as I could tell.

But then Mary Healy cleared up the mystery for us.

A Mr. Bantry White used to live in the house we had just left. Since this name was unknown to me prior to that moment, Sybil of course could not have gotten it from my unconscious mind prior to visiting the Donnybrook house. Were Wynan and White the same person, I wondered.

Another thing that struck me as peculiar was Sybil's insistence on going to a house *with an iron gate*. No such house was on my list but Sybil kept asking for it. When we arrived at Ballinguile, however, there was no iron gate within view; still, Sybil demanded to see it, sure it was part of this house.

I then learned from Mrs. Healy that she had had such an iron gate removed when she bought the house, and moved the entrance to where it is now, away from where the old iron gate once stood. Sybil again could not have known this consciously.

The new home of the Healy family was neat and functional, and Mrs. Healy a charming lady gifted with elaborate speech and a sense of proportion.

"There lived a Mr. Kerrigan there, a lawyer also," she said. "I think he is dead. We bought it from a Dr. Graham who died quite recently. But nobody has ever lived in that house *very long*. We left it for purely personal reasons, not because of any ghost, however."

"What about the cottage?"

"That was built by Dr. Graham for his gardener. That is of no age at all. A Mr. Barron is living in it now."

"Which staircase did you hear the footsteps on?" I asked.

"There are two, as there are two of everything in the house. My son-in-law and I bought it together, you see, and it was on the little staircase that I heard the footsteps. In the back of the house. The party sounds I heard, that was in the older house, too, in the back."

Where Sybil and I had heard the voices, I thought! Same spot, actually, and I did not realize it until now.

"Did you find any traces of older buildings on the spot?" I asked Mrs. Healy.

"There is supposed to have been a monastery on these grounds at one time," she explained; "only the well in the garden is left now. We still used the clear water from it, incidentally."

Later, Mrs. Healy's brother came and joined us. He listened quietly as I explained about the land business and the complaint of the ghost.

Both tenants prior to the Doctor had been lawyers, it turned out, and the difficulty about the land ownership underneath the house was quite real. If there had been some mistake, however, nothing could be done about it *now*. At least not without costly and extended search and litigation. And that, you will admit, even a ghost wouldn't want. Especially not a lawyer-ghost who is getting no fee out of it! I am sure that my explanation, that time had gone on, must have given the ghostly owner a chance to let go of it all, and since Mr. Lurie, the present owner, foresees that an apartment structure will soon replace the old house, there really is no point in worrying about a bit of land. *Caveat emptor!*

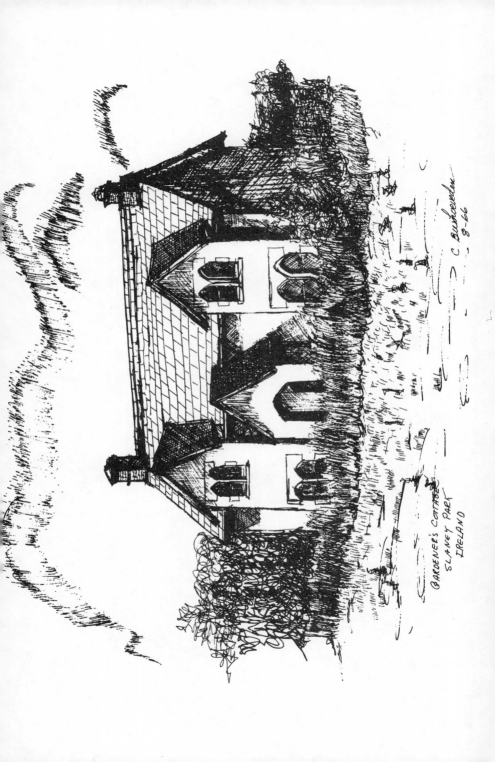

GARDENER'S COTTAGE
SLANEY PARK
IRELAND

C. Butterden
8-66

The Haunted Cottage

Lord Dunalley's charming secretary, Marie Rose, phoned to say she knew of a haunted house and would we be interested? A bonus case, I thought, one I had not heard of. It turned out that the people in question owned a haunted cottage on their grounds that they had been trying to rent, unsuccessfully, and this was a state of affairs they did not like. So they had the vicar in to exorcise whatever it was that caused everybody to leave in a hurry. The results of his endeavors were not yet final, but they thought as long as we were in the vicinity, why not have us have a go at it also?

Normally I don't compete with vicars, but I was so sure that religious exorcism only works if the ghost is religious that I accepted the bid. Consequently we hired a car with driver and left Dublin right after lunch, taking the southern road to a quiet country town called Baltinglass, in County Wicklow. The ride was pleasant, and we admired the scenery as well as the cows dotting it. For lunch we stopped in the village itself where we did pretty well considering the remoteness of the area. Then we started out for the house in what is called Slaney Park. The estate belongs to the Grogan family and is set in the middle of a spacious farm. John Grogan is a gentleman farmer and a practical man, and the cottage had him baffled.

When we arrived, I asked immediately to be taken to the suspicious cottage before he or his wife could tell us anything more. All I knew was that there was a haunted cottage and Thursday was particularly bad. It so happened that the day was also Thursday, so we set out in an expectant mood.

The cottage, about a mile away from the manor house, was a pleasant-looking gray stone house, two stories in all, set amid lush fields and farmland, with a wide view towards the rolling hills of Wicklow. Sybil did not know anything about it; in fact, she hardly knew where we were!

Immediately I took her inside, and the two of us wandered about the house while Catherine stayed with the Grogans to chat.

The house was in bad condition mainly from the birds which had gotten in through the many broken windows. But Mr. Grogan did not feel like fixing it up until he knew it was *safe*. We stopped in the downstairs part in front of an old fireplace.

"Are we in the right spot, Sybil?"

"No, I don't feel anything here. Let's go upstairs."

So we did, and Sybil stopped in the room to the right of the staircase.

"This is a very emotional place . . . death, I would think," she began her appraisal, "not a particularly pleasant one . . . sudden death."

"Do you feel any personal contact yet?"

"No, just a disagreeable, *unwanted* feeling."

"Man or woman?"

"Man."

"What period?"

"Sixty years ago."

"Is he still present?"

"Yes . . . the fight for whatever it was did not resolve anything."

"Meaning?"

"The death was in vain. For nothing."

"What does he want now?"

"What was unsolved then, still has to be solved, I think. Strange female influence has crept in. *Three people* . . . female influence in the house connected with the violence. The cause of it, I'd say."

"A woman is the cause of the violence?"

"Yes."

"Try to contact the one who is here and ask for his name and what he wants."

"The name that comes to me is *Drummond*. He doesn't really want to talk to us."

"Whom does he want to talk to then?"

"Wayne . . . a name like Wayne! Seems to me a *domestic* thing . . . something had to be hushed up, that's what it is . . . secretive. . . ."

I asked Sybil to convey our concern to the ghost that we were quite willing to help him in this matter. Sybil repeated my instructions in a low voice. The Grogans were downstairs chatting away about the farm meanwhile. They could not hear anything that went on upstairs.

"Elizabeth Wayne," Sybil said definitely now, "Elizabeth Wayne . . . that is the contact."

"What are his reasons?"

"He left the house . . . was driven away from the house . . . when he came back there were strangers here. Family trouble. This was his place to rest. Land is important, too. This is a place where many quarrels took place. Someone is unreasonable."

I proceeded to tell Drummond that he had passed over and should leave. Sybil seconded me.

"He's destructive," Sybil said. "Remember the name James Bryson . . . has something to do with this land. He goes from here to another place . . . there is another place if he can find it. . . ."

"Go outside where your loved ones await you," I intoned. "We've come to liberate you and bring you justice on the outside."

"It's not his time of day to be here," Sybil said. "He's gone now."

"What is the right time for this haunting?"

"We're almost on it. Summer. August 6th . . . has meaning."

I asked Sybil if there was anything else she felt about this case.

"There is another house," she replied. "Either it is one that once stood here or it is the house he is thinking of, *but there is a second house involved.*"

We left the cottage and drove back to the manor house, where the Grogans were comfortably ensconced in what was once a much bigger house, but which had been reduced somewhat when its top story had burned up some years ago. I decided to talk first to John Grogan, and do this in the presence of Sybil, since she had already done her psychic part.

John Grogan is a man in his early thirties, of medium height, who inherited the property from his father just a few years ago, prior to which he had a farm of his own nearby, which he still owns.

"All I know," Grogan began slowly, "is that there was a Scottish head gardener. His marriage wasn't particularly happy; his wife's sister came over to stay, and he had an affair with her.

"The wife found out and there was unpleasantness. Finally the sister decided to go, and the wife took the sister to put her on the train, at Baltinglass, and when she got back to the cottage, the house was locked. She could not get in. She came down to my great-grandmother, and she went up and broke in the door of the cottage. She found the gardener had committed suicide by hanging himself on the bannister there. *Upstairs.*"

Mr. Grogan did not know the gardener's name. However, Drummond *is* a Scottish name.

"After that, anyone who had ever been at the house was aware that something was wrong. Knocking on the door Thursday nights, for instance. Nobody would stay there. My father couldn't keep anyone there very long. They complained about this funny feeling that they were not alone."

"How long ago did this tragedy occur?" I asked.

"Around the turn of the century."

How right Sybil had been, saying it happened sixty years ago!

"What about yourself? Any experiences in the cottage?"

"Well, on one or two occasions, I've had the feeling that there was somebody else around. That I've been watched. That was in the daytime and it never worried me much."

"Is there anything of this kind in the manor house?"

"No, nothing at all. The house came into the possession of my family in 1755, and there was a house here then; it belonged to the Crosby family before my family came here, but there was never anything unusual here in the main house."

I thanked John Grogan for his help and turned to his wife.

"I wouldn't go much into the cottage," she began, "because my father-in-law told me about it, but there was an unpleasant feeling about that cottage."

"Were you ever in it alone?"

"Yes, once. I had the distinct feeling that someone was watching me."

"What else do you know about the cottage?"

"An old man called Hanley lived there some time ago, and he said he knew there was something there, but he did not mind it. On one occasion, however, he put a cup of tea down, and when he turned his back and tried to pick it up a moment later, it was gone. That was about ten, fifteen years ago."

"Who was the last person to live in the cottage?"

"A Miss Willoughby. She left, because she could not stand living there."

"What did she tell you?"

"She heard knocking Thursday evenings, so much so she used to always go out on Thursday evenings to avoid it."

"And before Miss Willoughby?"

"That was Hanley. Then there was an electrician, and he

moved out too. We've only been here since last November, you see, and some of these things were before our time."

"Quite so," I said. "Do you know of any traditional gossip in the village concerning the cottage?"

"They talk principally about knocking at ten o'clock on Thursday nights. They never talk to me about it, but one hears these things."

John Grogan came over once more.

"This man Hanley had a daughter," he said, "and he was away—you see, he was a stone mason and very often he was away—and the daughter got very seriously ill there; she was absolutely terrified by the presence and the noises."

I thanked the Grogans and assured them that to the best of my knowledge and experience, the cottage ought to be about ready for a new paint job. So that the next gardener could move in.

Again, Sybil Leek, without foreknowledge, had pinpointed the area of disturbance, the fact of violent death, and the human triangle—the year of the tragedy—and the futility of his act. As for the names, they are being checked out now. But to the Grogans it really does not matter what their ghost was called. Just so long as the cottage is empty again.

One thing that had baffled me about this case, however, was Sybil's insistence that there was another, earlier house on the spot where the gardener's cottage now stands. John Grogan had emphatically denied that there had been such a house.

A few weeks after our visit, he was clearing and excavating foundations for a new hay barn when he came across the foundations of an earlier house!

WESTOWN HOUSE
COUNTY DUBLIN
IRELAND

C. Biedermeier
8-66

A Perfect Place for Hallowe'en

THE PERFECT PLACE FOR A HALLOWE'EN CELEBRATION IS A totally ruined mansion or greathouse called Westownhouse, near Naul, north of Dublin. What makes it such a fine place for shivers is its eerie appearance, the stark ruins of a once great mansion, reduced to a shell, the lush wilderness of the vegetation that has since shot up around and through it and that makes a visit a matter of great hazard to life, limb, and certainly hats.

About two miles off the road, past a modest gamekeeper's lodge, the estate seems abandoned and the once well-kept gardens are in shambles; the road gets narrower and stonier as one progresses into the green. Eventually, one has to bend low to walk under the branches of trees that have long entwined their arms, forming a natural roof over the path. It is never dry under these trees, for the soil retains its moisture beyond belief. Around a curve one comes upon the shell of the greathouse staring into the landscape like a blind giant. Beyond the house there are extensive stables, or rather there were, for they are now also nothing more than walls overgrown with grass and plant life. Behind the stables, there is the high wall that surrounds the entire estate.

The area, though only an hour's ride from Dublin, is very lonely, and as so often in Ireland, sparsely populated.

I first heard about Westownhouse from a young couple in Dublin. She is a law secretary, with a sister in America through whom she had heard of me, and her friend is a technical salesman working for a large machinery company. I was asked to shield their identity, but they came to see me at Jury's Hotel in Dublin and I found them both rational, personable people, around thirty years of age, or thereabouts, and a bit shy about their experiences at Westownhouse.

In one of their recent meanderings around the countryside, they had come upon the ruins of the house and decided to explore it. Both were possessed by an interest in antiquities and historical relics and this house attracted them. They knew nothing of its history at the time. As they were walking through the ruins of the mansion towards the stables, the girl suddenly felt a presence with her. She looked around, but her friend was nowhere near her. When he rejoined her later, she told him of her strange and fearsome feelings.

"I'm glad you felt it too," he finally confessed, and then explained what had happened to him as he was standing amid the masonry alone.

"Someone was breathing down my neck, directly behind me," he said slowly, "and of course you were not with me at that point, so it could not have been you."

The girl confirmed this, and they decided they had better get out of there before it was totally dark!

Since Naul was on our way to Dundalk, it was easy for us to have a look at the place. Sybil as usual had no idea where we were off to, and dutifully she crawled through the underbrush with us as we set out on foot to reach the house, leaving car and driver farther down the road.

I had scarcely set foot on the stone steps of the greathouse when Sybil disappeared. A moment later, she returned from the thicket telling me there was nothing at all of a psychic nature in the greathouse, but would I please follow her *to the stable area.*

This I did, and in back of the house we stopped in what had once been the paddock, with bronze knobs still protruding from the walls.

"When I was at this spot before, I had a monastic feeling and a distinct impression of hearing bells," Sybil explained.

"Bells?"

"Bells," Sybil confirmed, "and there is something very tragic here."

Of course, an earlier building had undoubtedly occupied the site, for judging from what I saw of the house, it belonged to the 18th century and later.

"This is an area that was the scene of a tremendous escape," Sybil continued, "—a person tried to escape but did not succeed. There are two different levels here and I think the monastic level is the earlier one."

"Stay with the later level," I requested. "This escape, how long ago was that?"

"1926."

"Who is the person trying to escape?"

"Trehayne or Trelane . . . a name like that. He was killed along this wall." She pointed to the rear of the stables. "Four people were concerned . . ."

"After he was killed, was there any difficulty about it?" I asked.

"There are repercussions. This killing does not solve anything but starts something."

"Is this person still here?"

"Yes."

"Why?"

"He does not know . . . contact difficult. The other period, religious atmosphere, intrudes."

"Who is the victim of the killing?"

"He has an administrative position."

"Who was involved here . . . what was at stake?"

"A group of people . . . I get the word Dail—D-a-i-l."

"Dail means parliament," I said. "What about it?"

"It is somehow connected with this."

"Let us get back to the person who was killed here. Who did the killing?"

"Not people in uniform. Trehayne is the victim, a man. Willard did the killing. Robert Willard or Willet. He killed him because he thought Trehayne was treacherous to the movement ... to the people who met here. . . . Trehayne did not belong to the Dial. . . . Willet went to London. . . ."

"Was the killing reported publicly?"

"No, as an accident. He fell . . . ."

"How was he killed?"

"With a gun."

"Are both still here or only one?"

"Both here, but Trehayne is the one who stays here. He waits for the others to fetch him."

When Sybil said that the murder victim could see her, I instructed her to approach him mentally, with an offer of aid.

"He need not stay on," I intoned, "for we know what he died for. No need to wait—everything is understood."

"It's dark," Sybil said, interpreting for the ghost.

"It's light outside where your people and friends are," I replied and continued to urge him to go.

"He's gone now," Sybil said, and added, with some astonishment in her voice, "and the bells are ringing!"

Could it be that the monks of that earlier period were celebrating the delivery of a lost soul?

"There is a coat of arms," Sybil said, "three trees on the left, and a bird on the right; it's connected with this house."

"The man who was here, how does he connect with this house?"

"A visitor."

We walked back to the waiting car and I stopped at the gatekeeper's lodge, where the wife of the gatekeeper had just returned from fetching water in buckets. There was no plumbing whatever on the grounds.

"I don't know very much about the place," she began.

"Originally a family named Hussey lived here; the last people who had it were the Martins. I've only been here five years, so I really don't know too much about what went on here earlier. I'm Mrs. Hegan."

The land had been divided up and the house let go, she explained, and the lodge she and her family occupied was sub-leased from the owner of that part of the land.

I thanked Mrs. Hegan and we took our leave, heading towards Dundalk.

Then I tried to piece the story together, fragmentary though it was.

The Dublin couple had made some inquiries after their har-rowing experience in the ruins. It seems that a poacher had been caught on the grounds near the house and shot by one of the men in the house. Ever since then—and this happened in the 1920's—the gatehouse keeper had been disturbed by a presence, until he himself quit and the house was abandoned.

Sybil had correctly identified the area in which the killing had taken place, the fact that it was a male victim, that he was shot, and the period of the killing; she had identified him as merely a visitor and the other man as a man in an administrative position.

Was this really a poacher being shot in exercise of an ancient but certainly severe prerogative? Or was the guise of the poacher adopted to cover another reason for the murder?

Although we will never be sure now that the ghost is gone, it is comforting to know that Westownhouse is safe for any Hallowe'en party bent on a visit now—the spooks they may conjure up will merely be their own.

The Haunted Rectory

THE FIRST TIME I HEARD OF THE HAUNTED RECTORY OF CARL-ingford was in August of 1965, when its owner, Ernest McDowell, approached me on the advice of an American friend who knew of my work.

"I own an old rectory which is haunted. If you are interested I will show you over the house with pleasure."

Subsequently, I ascertained that Mr. McDowell was a man of standing and intelligence, and his report was to be taken seriously. I arranged for us to go up to the Dundalk area in late July of 1966. By this time, two editors from the German fashion magazine *Constanze*, Mr. and Mrs. Peter Rober, had decided to join us for a firsthand report on my methods, and also to act as neutral observers and arbiters should my camera yield some supernormal photographs. For this purpose, an elaborate system of safeguards was devised by Mr. Rober. It consisted of his bringing from Hamburg the very sensitive film I normally use for the purpose and personally inserting it in my Zeiss camera, which he kept in his own possession until we were ready to visit the house in question.

After he had filled the camera with film, he sealed it with string and red sealing wax, so that I could not possibly manipulate the camera or the film inside without breaking the seal. By this method he was in a firm position to attest to the fact that nobody had tampered with my camera and to further attest that if supernormal results were obtained, they had been obtained genuinely and not by fraud. I was happy to oblige the German editors, since an article in that materialistic country, dealing in a positive way with psychic phenomena, would be an important step forward.

The Robers arrived on a hot Saturday evening at Jury's Hotel, and the following morning we set out for Dundalk in one of those huge Princess cars that can seat six comfortably. We arrived at Ballymascanlon Hotel north of Dundalk by lunch time; I had chosen this comfortable inn as our headquarters.

The former Plunkett residence, now fully modernized and really an up-to-date hostelry in every sense of the word, has beginnings going back to the 9th century, although the house itself is only a hundred years old. This area abounds in "giants' tombs" and other pre-Christian relics, and was the center of the Scanlan family for many centuries. Later it belonged to the Cistercian monks of Mellifont, a ruin we had visited the year before when we crossed the river Boyne.

As soon as Mrs. Irene Quinn, the hotel's spunky owner, had settled us into our rooms, we made plans. I put in a telephone call to Ernest McDowell and a pleasant, well-modulated voice answered me on the other end of the line. He was indeed ready for the expedition; within an hour he had driven over from his own home, a farm south of Dundalk called Heynestown, and we sat down in the comfortable lounge of Ballymascanlon Hotel to go over his experiences in detail.

"Let us start with the history of the house, as far as you know it at this moment," I asked McDowell, a pleasant-looking, well-dressed young man in his fortieth year whose profession was that of a painter, although he helped his brother run their farm as required. By and large Ernest McDowell was a gentleman farmer, but more gentleman than farmer, and rather on the shy side.

"The house was built in the 17th century," he began. "It was then a private house, a mansion that belonged to the Stannus family, before it was bought by the Church of Ireland for a rectory. The builder of the newer portion was the grandfather of the celebrated Sadler's Wells ballerina Ninette de Valois. I bought it in 1960."

"Have you moved in yet?"

"I haven't really . . . the house is empty, except of course for the ghosts."

"Ah yes," I said. "How large a house is it?"

"Twenty-two rooms in all. Nobody has lived there since I bought it, though."

"When was your first visit to the house, after you had acquired it?"

"I went up there every week to see if it was all right."

"Was it?"

"Well, yes, but one summer afternoon, in 1963—it was early September, I recall—my brother and I were at the rectory. My brother was out cutting corn, and I was mowing the lawn. It was rather a hot evening and I thought I was getting a cold. I was very busy, though, and I just happened to look up, towards the door, when I noticed moving towards the door *a figure of a girl in a red dress.*

"The motor of the lawnmower was not in good repair and it had bothered me, and I was taken aback by what I saw. It was a red velvet dress she wore, and before I could see her face, she just vanished!"

"Did she look solid?"

"Solid."

"Did she cast a shadow?"

"No."

"Did she touch the ground?"

"Yes."

"Did you see her shoes?"

"There wasn't time. I started from the ground up, and the red dress was the first thing I noticed."

"About that face?"

"I couldn't make it out."

"What period would you say the dress belonged to?"

"It was Edwardian, long."

"What did you do after she vanished?"

"I looked towards the gate—the gate that lets you into the grounds from the road—and coming in the gate was a clergyman with a very high collar, and he vanished, too!"

"Do you recall anything else about him?"

"He wore a rather out-of-date outfit, and a hat."

"What time of day was it?"

"About five p. m."

I thought about this ghostly encounter of two restless spirits for a moment, before continuing my questioning of the chief witness.

"Did they react to each other in any way?"

"I should say there was some bond between the two; there was a connection."

"Did you see anything else?"

"No, just the two figures."

"Did your brother see anything?"

"No. But Canon Meissner, who lived at the house for some time, saw the same girl in one of the rooms. She appeared to him on a separate occasion."

"How long ago?"

"About twenty years ago. He described her as a young girl who appeared near his bed and then just disappeared."

"Disconcerting for a Canon, I'd say. What else can you tell me about the haunted rectory?"

"Helen Meissner, his daughter, was in the dining room one night, with the door open, alone, when the other door, on the other end of the room, suddenly started to vibrate as if someone were trying hard to push it open. It opened by itself and the dog with her stood and stared at whatever came through the door, its hackles rising, and then it ran for its life.

"Then, too, Mrs. Meissner, the Canon's wife, and Helen heard footsteps on the backstairs one night. The steps started on the bottom of the stairs and went right up, past them, as they were standing on both sides of the stairs; but they did not see anything. This was about fifteen years ago when Meissner was Rector and lived at the house with his family.

"My sister-in-law, who is very sensitive, went through the house only two weeks ago, and she claimed that the back part of the house gave her a very uncomfortable feeling. She owned a house in Kent, England, that was haunted and we both felt it. I suppose we are both psychic to a degree, since I've on occasion felt things."

"What sort of things?" I asked. I always like to get a full picture of my witnesses to evaluate their testimony. If they have had ghostly experiences prior to the one under investigation, it would indicate mediumistic faculties in them.

"My brother and sister-in-law had bought a house in Kildare and I stayed there one night, and for no reason at all, I sat up in bed from a deep sleep, and I clearly heard both locks on the doors in the room click. But I was quite alone."

"To your knowledge, is there any record of any unhappy incident in this house?" I asked, getting back to the haunted rectory.

"No, it has a very happy atmosphere. Only when I go into it sometime, I feel as if there were people in it, yet it is obviously empty. It seems alive to me. Of course, I have heard footsteps in the corridors when I was quite alone in the house. That was mainly upstairs. It's a passage that runs up one stairway and around the house and down the other staircase. The only thing smacking of tragedy I know of was the coachman losing a child in the gatehouse that burned down, but that was not in the house itself."

"Is there any tradition or popular rumor that might refer to the apparitions of the clergyman and the girl in the red dress?"

"None whatever."

Thus it was that all members of our party had no foreknowledge of any event connected with the haunted house, no names, or anything more than what Ernest McDowell had just told us. Sybil, of course, was nowhere near us at this point, since she was to join us only after the preliminaries had been done with.

The Germans took it all down with their tape recorders, and it was for their benefit that I made the point of our total "innocence" as far as facts and names were concerned.

"What is the house called now?" I asked.

"Mount Trevor," Mr. McDowell replied. "It was originally built by the Trevors, a very well-known country family. They also built the town of Rostrevor, across Carlingford Lough."

"Are there any chairs in the house now?" I finally asked, since Sybil had to sit down *somewhere* for her trance. McDowell assured me he had thought of it and brought one chair—just one —to the otherwise empty house.

When we arrived at the house after a pleasant drive of about fifteen minutes, Peter Rober gave me back my camera, fully sealed now, and I took pictures at random downstairs and upstairs, and Catherine joined me in taking some shots also, with the same camera.

We entered the grounds, where the grass stood high, and McDowell led us into the house by a side entrance, the only door now in use, although I was immediately impressed that a larger door facing the other way must at one time have existed.

The house is pleasantly situated atop a knoll gently sloping down towards the water of Carlingford Lough, with trees dotting the landscape and sheep grazing under them, giving the place a very peaceful feeling. In back of the house lay a kitchen garden, beyond which the ruined towers of ancient Carlingford Abbey could be seen in the distance. Across the road from the garden gate was the Catholic church house of Carlingford.

The hall was rather small; to the left, the staircase mentioned in the ghostly accounts immediately led to the upper story, while to the right of the door a short passage took us into the large downstairs corner room, where we decided to remain. Large windows all around gave the room sufficient illumination, and there was a fireplace in the rear wall. Next to it stood the lone chair McDowell had mentioned.

Sybil joined us now inside the house and I hurried to get her first clairvoyant impressions as they occurred.

"Something connected with the period of 1836," she said immediately, poking about the rooms. "I have two names . . . as we came in the name *Woodward* came to me, and the other is *Devine or Divine.* Something like that. Peculiar name, I think."

"Please don't analyze it," I warned, "just let it come. *I'll* do the analyzing."

"Woodward and Devine," Sybil repeated. "These names have some meaning in this house. Also, a hall of imprisonment. Someone was imprisoned, I feel."

We followed Sybil, who slowly walked from room to room. Catherine helped me carry the tape recorder and camera, Ernest McDowell following behind looking excited, and three friends of his whose presence he felt might be useful. They were two ladies sharing a house at Ardee, both of them very psychic. Mrs. Bay John and Pat MacAllister had brought a young ward named Julian with them. I secretly hoped there weren't any *poltergeists* lurking about under the circumstances!

Later, Mrs. MacAllister mentioned seeing a face as if etched onto the wall in the very room upstairs where I took some psychic pictures, though of course I did not know they would turn out to be unusual at the time I took them. I never know these things beforehand.

We were still on the ground floor and Sybil was investigating the rear section, the oldest part of the house. There were some iron bars outside the window of the rather dank room, giving it a very heavy prison-like feeling. It was the original kitchen area.

"Someone was *made to* stay upstairs," Sybil said now, "and I have gooseflesh on my forearms now." We walked up the stairs and I confirmed the latter observation.

Finally we found ourselves in a room about the middle of the upper story, and Sybil came to a halt.

"I feel I want to run away from this room," she observed. "It's a panic-stricken feeling. Someone wants to get away from here; the name Devine comes again here. Someone is hiding here, and then there is imprisonment. Is there a prison somewhere here?

Several people are held. This is away from the house, however."

"Is there a presence here?" I asked as I always do when we are at the center of uncanny activities.

"Yes, several. The period is 1836. The strongest presence is someone in brown. A man. There is a connection with business. There are three people here, but of the same period. There is no overlapping of periods here. The main person hiding in this room or forcibly kept here went from here and was hanged, with other people. This was a man. Perhaps we should go downstairs now."

We followed Sybil's advice and repaired to the downstairs parlor.

"Father Devine . . . should not have left the church for business," Sybil suddenly mumbled. "Someone says that about him. I feel him around, though."

Now I placed Sybil in the one chair we had and the rest of us formed a circle around her as best we could. It was about the same time, five o'clock, as the time of the haunting and I was prepared for *anything*.

Presently, Sybil showed all signs of deep trance. My German friends were riveted to the floor, Mrs. Rober clutching the microphone and Mr. Rober taking dozens of pictures with his Rolleiflex camera. The tension mounted as Sybil's lips started to move, though no word came at first through them. Gradually, I coaxed the spirit to take firmer possession of my medium's body and to confide in us who had come as friends.

"Who are you?" I said softly. The voice now emanating from Sybil was hesitant and weak, not at all like Sybil's normal voice.

"Aileen," the voice murmered.

I could hardly hear her, but my tape recorder picked up every breath.

"Aileen Woodward," the ghost said.

"Is this your house?"

"We live here . . . where is he? Where is he? Robert!"

"Whom are you seeking?"

"Devaine . . . Robert Devaine . . . speak slightly . . . my husband . . . be quiet . . . where is he?"

I wondered if she wanted me to keep my voice down so that I would not give her away to some pursuers.

"Where is Robert?" I asked, trying to reverse the line of questioning.

"Where is he, where is he?" she cried instead, becoming more and more upset and the tears, real tears, streaming down Sybil's usually tranquil face.

I calmed her as best I could, promising to help her find Robert, if I could.

"When did you first come to this house?" I asked quietly, while the sobbing continued.

The faces around me showed the great emotions that seemed to have been transferred from the ghostly girl to the witnesses. Not a word was spoken.

At this point, the tape had to be turned over. Unfortunately, it slipped out of our hands and it was several seconds before I started to record again. During those moments I tried to explore her family connections more fully.

Who was Robert and who were his people? Who was Robert's father?

"In the Church," she replied, quieter now.

"Does he like you?" I wanted to know.

There was a moment of quiet reflection before she answered. "No."

"Why not?"

"The Church must not marry!"

"Is Robert a priest?"

"Shhh!" she said quickly. "Don't speak!"

"I don't quite understand . . . how does religion enter the picture?"

"Changer," she mumbled, indicating that someone had changed his faith.

"Are you and Robert of the same religion?" I now asked.

"Don't ask it."

"Are you Catholic?"

Utter silence was my answer.

I pleaded with her for more information so I could help her

locate Robert. In vain; she would not budge on this question. Finally, she confused me with her enemies.

"You took him . . . I'm going for a walk now . . . follow . . . down the hill . . . just a walk . . . to see if he comes. . . ."

"If I get you to see Robert again, will you promise to do as I tell you?" I asked.

"I promise nothing," the frightened ghost replied. "You betray him . . . how do I know you're a friend?"

"You have to trust me if I am to help you."

"I don't trust."

Now I gently told her the truth about herself, the time that had come and gone since 1836 and why she could not stay on in this house.

"Don't speak so loud . . . you drive me mad . . . I'm going for a walk in the garden . . ." she said, trying to ignore the light of truth piercing her self-inflicted prison. But it did not work. The door of reality had been opened to her. In a moment she was gone.

Sybil reopened her eyes, confused at first as to where she was. I then asked her to take some fresh air outside the house, since the rain that had come down during part of our séance had now stopped and the countryside was back to its glorious Irish freshness.

With Sybil outside, I turned once more to the owner of the house and asked whether he had ever heard the names Woodward, Aileen, and Devine or Devaine before in connection with the house or area.

"The only thing I know is that Canon Meissner told me that this house was once occupied by a French family named Devine. Since Canon Meissner had the house from 1935 onward, this must have been before his time."

"The girl speaks of a clergyman, and you saw a clergyman ghost, is that correct?"

"Yes," McDowell nodded, "but he wore black, not brown."

In the time we had lost through the tape change, the ghost had described herself as 16 years of age, wearing a red dress, and the dates 1836 and 1846 both were given. Sybil, of course, had no knowledge of McDowell's experience with the girl in the red velvet dress.

I asked Mr. McDowell to look in the local records for confirmation of some of the names and information that had come through the medium. Offhand, none of it was known to those present, so that confirmation would have to await further research.

We returned to Ballymascanlon Hotel, where the eager German journalist had made an appointment with a local photographer so that he could get my films developed while we were still on location, and if there was anything on the negatives that had not been visible to the naked eye, one could make immediate use of the information. I never anticipated anything of this sort, but one can't know these things in advance either. As it turned out, there *were* two pictures in the batch, taken by Catherine and me with my sealed camera, that showed the same mirror-like effects I had observed on the photographs taken in June Havoc's haunted townhouse in New York and in the haunted trailer of Rita Atlanta, near Boston. Wherever there is present in a room a haunted area, represented by a magnetic field or a coldspot sometimes, such an area occasionally shows up on film with mirror-like effects; that is, reflections of objects in the room occur that could not have occurred under ordinary conditions, there being no mirror or other reflecting surface near.

Peter Rober was clearly elated, showing his pleasure about as much as his North German nature permitted him to. There was still another picture that represented a puzzle to us: in the haunted room upstairs where Helen Meissner had seen the door open by its own volition, Catherine took a picture in what seemed to both of us an empty room. We clearly recall that the doors were both shut. Yet, to our amazement, on the picture the door to the left is quite plainly ajar!

Ernest McDowell suggested we talk to the Meissners firsthand, and the following morning, Mr. and Mrs. Rober and I drove across the border to Northern Ireland, where the Meissners now live in a little town called Warrenpoint.

Mrs. Meissner turned out to be a friendly, talkative lady who readily agreed to tell us what had happened to them during their tenancy at the rectory.

"We lived there twenty-five years, and we left the house in 1960," she began her recollections. "We did not notice anything unusual about the house at first, perhaps because we were so glad to get the house.

"Part of the house was almost Queen Anne period, the rest Georgian. We had two indoor maids and we took our gardener with us, too. Everybody was happy. We did lots of entertaining and life was very pleasant. Then I noticed that local people never came to the rectory *in the evening*. They always made an excuse. Finally, I was informed that there was a ghost in the house. It was supposed to have been the ghost of a sea captain who lived here originally and was lost at sea. The older portion of the house was where he had lived, they said. I never was able to find out anything more than that about this sea captain, however. I was a skeptic myself and went gaily about my business. Then summer came, and I used to be outdoors as late as one could. Several evenings, *something white* passed me, something big, and yet I never heard a sound. I thought this very strange, of course, and wondered if it was a white owl. But there was no sound of wings. Gradually I got to rather expect this phenomenon."

"Any particular time of day?" I interjected.

"At dusk. Outside. And then I saw it from the window. But it had no form, yet I knew it was white. I saw it often, and never a sound."

"After that, did you have any further adventures in the house?" I asked.

"We had a visit from the sister of Ninette de Valois, and she was very interested in the house because it was an ancestor of hers who had owned it. He was a Colonel Stannus. At the same time we had another visitor, a young man from Dublin. The lady and her husband had come rather late in the evening; they were staying at Rostrevor Hotel, and they wanted to see over Carlingford Rectory, and we thought it was rather late in the evening for that, so we asked them to come the next day. At that time the young man from Dublin was here also, but he and the lady had never met.

"When he looked at the lady, he became suddenly white as a sheet. I wondered if he was ill, but he said no, so we moved on to a room that we always regarded as a guest room. The young man from Dublin had often stayed in that room before. But when we entered the room, the lady exclaimed that she had been in that room before! Of course she hadn't.

"The young fellow from Dublin still looked very shaken, so I took him downstairs to one side and said, What is wrong with you?

"Finally he told me.

" 'It's the most extraordinary thing,' he said to me. 'That lady is the ghost.'

" 'What ghost?' I asked.

" 'Often when I slept in that room,' he explained, 'I have been awakened by the feeling of a presence in the room. When I looked up, I saw the face of that lady!'

"What struck me as odd was that he felt something strange immediately upon meeting her and she felt something equally strange about having been to that room before when in fact she hadn't.

"Later, at tea, she asked me if I believed in the transmigration of souls."

The young man, whose name is Ronny Musgrave, evidently was reminded by the lady's appearance of the ghost's, I felt, but that would still not explain *her* reaction to the room, unless she had clairvoyantly foreseen her trip to Carlingford and was now realizing it!

"I've spent so much time in that house," Mrs. Meissner continued, "but I never felt I was alone. My husband's experience was different from mine. He had fallen asleep. He awoke, feeling that there was someone in the room. He thought it was an evil presence and he made the sign of the cross. Then it disappeared. I always thought the presence was female. I've heard footsteps, too. But I never feared this ghost. To me, it was pleasant."

I tried to piece together the past history of the house. Prior to 1932 when the Meissners moved in, there was a rector named Aughmuty there; before that the Reverend Bluett, before him his father-in-law, a Mr. Mailer, and that brings us back to the 19th century, when the Stannus family owned the place. It was just a private house then.

Mrs. Meissner did not recognize any of the names obtained during the trance, incidentally.

While she went to fetch her octogenarian husband to supplement some of the data for us, I had a talk with the daughter, now the widowed Mrs. Thompson, who had come over to the house to see us.

"We had a cocker spaniel," she began, "and the dog was with me in that upstairs room. There was a big mirror there then, and as I looked into it, I saw the door at the far end of the room open by itself, and then close again slowly. The dog got up and snarled and growled, but I saw nothing. That was the only experience that I had, but it was enough for me."

Canon Meissner is a lively and kind man who readily answered my questions as best he knew. None of the names rang a bell with him, as far as churchmen were concerned, and as for private origins, he did not really have the sources in his library. He recommended we take it up with Trinity College in Dublin where there are extensive records. The house had become a rectory about 1870 or 1871, he explained, and was directly purchased from the Stannus family at that time. They had built the newer part onto the already existing old portion.

I started to examine the two heavy books the Canon had brought with him from his study.

No Devine or Devaine showed up in the lists of rectors of Carlingford.

In *The Alumni of Trinity College*, London, Williams and

Norgate, 1924, on page 227, column 1, I found the following entry:

> Devine, Charles, admitted to Trinity, November 4, 1822, age 20 [thus born 1802]; son of John Devine, born County Louth.

That, of course, was the right area, for Carlingford was at that time the principal town in the county.

I further found a listing of "Robert Woodward, graduated Trinity, November 5, 1821, aged 16, son of Henry Woodward. M.A. 1832," on page 94 of the same work.

It seemed extraordinary that we had located two names given in trance by Sybil Leek, and that both names were of the right period claimed and in the right location. But the search was far from finished.

While I was trying to get some corroboration from the local librarian at Dundalk—without success—the German editors packed up and left for Hamburg. I left instructions with Ernest McDowell as to what I needed, and then the three of us, my wife and I and Sybil, went on to the western part of Ireland. There we parted company and Sybil went to her home in the south of England while we returned to New York.

On August 2, 1966, Sybil had a trance-like dream at her house at Ringwood, Hants. In this dream state she saw herself walking back and forth between the rectory and the ruined abbey. There was a girl who had come from some other place and had been waiting a long time for a man to join her. He had been in India. The girl was terribly upset and said that she had married the man but it was not legal and she had to find a Catholic priest to marry them because the whole thing was making her ill. He did not want to be married by a priest because he was a Protestant and his family would cut him off without any money.

He had left her because of her insistence on being married again, but she loved him and wanted to persuade him to agree to being married by a priest. She had been in England, and he told her to come to Ireland to Carlingford, where he could meet her, but he had not turned up. She had to find a priest who would keep the marriage secret, and this was not easy, as everyone said the marriage had to be written down in a book.

The girl claimed that "everything" could be found in the *Yelverton papers* in Dublin. Sybil was sure there was a Court case called the Yelverton case about the 1840-1850 period. But then things in the dream-like state got a bit confused as she found herself drifting in and out of the house, sometimes walking to the Abbey, talking to a priest, then back to the house, which at that time seemed furnished; and the gateway Sybil saw at the back of the house, not where it is now. The girl seemed to be staying with friends; she did not live at Carlingford permanently and indeed went on from there.

That was on August 2nd; on the third, Sybil again "dreamt" exactly the same sequence, which again culminated in the search for the Yelverton case papers. But the dream was more vivid this time; in the morning Sybil found that she had gotten up in the middle of the night, taken off her nightgown and put on a long evening dress, and then gone back to bed in it. She had the distinct feeling of wearing the same kind of clothes this girl wore in the 1840's. The girl said in all her moving around she could not get the right clothes to be married in and would have to buy more. The girl seemed to have an accent and spoke Italian and French in between a lot of crying and sniffling, and she seemed familiar to Sybil.

The latter was only too logical, since Sybil had been her instrument of communication, but we had not until now discussed the details of the case or her trance with Sybil; consequently she could not have known about the religious problem, for instance.

That was a monumental week for this case, for on the following day, and quite independently of Sybil's impressions, Ernest McDowell had come across the needed corroboration in a rare local chronicle. In a work entitled *County Families of the United Kingdom, 1800*, the family named Woodhouse, of Omeath Park, near Carlingford, was listed.

Omeath is the next village after Carlingford and quite close to it.

John Woodhouse, born October 6, 1804, married to Mary Burleigh, June 10, 1834; nine children, the fourth of which was Adeline Elizabeth. Now the Irish would pronounce Adeline rather like Ad'lin, and what I had heard from Sybil's entranced lips sounded indeed like A'lin, or Ad'lin!

The Woodhouse family claimed descent from the Wood-houses of Norfolk, England; thus Sybil's reference to the girl having been to England might fit. Perhaps she had gone to visit relatives.

Further in the same source, there is a listing also for the family Woodward of Drumbarrow. A Robert Woodward, born June 20, 1805, is given, whose father was Henry Woodward. Robert Woodward, according to the source, married one Esther Wood-ward and had two sons and three daughters. This marriage took place in 1835. This is the same man also listed in the register of Trinity College.

The similarity of the names Woodward and Woodhouse may have been confusing to the ghostly girl. One was presumably her maiden name and the other that of her husband's family.

Unfortunately, we don't have the birth dates for Adeline. But if her father was married only in 1834, she could not very well have married Robert in 1836 or even 1846. If she was six-teen at the time as she claimed in trance, and if she had been born somewhere between 1835 and 1845, we get to the period of around 1850-1860 as the time in which her tragic liaison with Robert might have taken place. But this is speculation.

What we do know concretely is this: nobody, including Sybil Leek, ever heard of a man named Devine, a girl named Adeline Woodhouse, a man named Robert Woodward, before this in-vestigation took place. These names were not in anyone's un-conscious mind at the time of our visit to Carlingford Rectory. Yet these people existed in the very area in which we had been and at the approximate time when the ghost had been active there in her lifetime. How can that be explained by any other reasoning than true communication with a restless departed soul?

What were the relationships between the girl in the red velvet dress and her Robert, and how did the father fit into this and which one was the clergyman? Was Devine the clergyman who destroyed their marriage or did he help them? It seems to me that it is his ghost Ernest McDowell observed. Is there a feeling of guilt present that kept him in these surroundings perhaps?

At any rate, the rectory has been quiet ever since our visit and Ernest McDowell is thinking of moving in soon. That is, if we don't buy the place from him. For the peaceful setting is tempting and the chance of ever encountering the girl in the red velvet dress, slim. Not that any of us would have minded.

ROSS HOUSE
MAYO.
IRELAND

C. Buchheimzier
8-66

Ghost Hunting in County Mayo

R OSS HOUSE STANDS ON A BLUFF LOOKING DIRECTLY OUT INTO
Clew Bay, halfway between Westport and Newport, and
in about as nice a position as anyone would wish. From its windows you can see the many islands dotting the bay, one of which
is part of the demesne of the house, and the lush green park in
back of the house gives a nice contrast to the salty clime of the
frontal portion. All in all, it is a house worthy of its owner, Major
M. J. Blackwell, retired officer formerly in the British Army
and nowadays in business in Chicago, U.S.A., as the second, but
by no means minor, half of the celebrated firm of Crosse & Blackwell.

I shan't tell you how to get to Ross House, for it is not easy,
what with Western Irish roads, but then there is no need to go
there unless you're invited, is there?—and that might well be,
for the Major is hospitality personified and his house always
rings with the laughter of young relatives and their friends
come over for a holiday.

The house itself is exquisitely furnished in both its stories, the
rooms being large and modern, for the house it not too ancient;
the broad Georgian staircase is a masterpiece unto itself, and,
as I found out later, it also attracted one of the resident ghosts
frequently. But about this in good time.

I first heard about Ross House from the Major's young nephew, Edwin Stanley, an American living in New Jersey. Mr. Stanley had read my books and thought it might be worth my while to visit the house. Subsequently Major Blackwell himself invited us to come, and it was July 28, 1966, when we finally made it, driving up from Leenane, where we were staying.

As soon as we had met the brood of youngsters assembled in the house, and the two baby cats, I repaired with the Major to his study upstairs, where we could get down to *ghost* business.

"Let's talk about the house first," I began. "When was it built?"

"It is a Georgian house as you can see, but prior to that, there had been another house here of which we are not quite certain, to the back of the present house. It is on the oldest maps. I inherited it from my mother, and it goes back in her family for quite a long time. My mother's side of the family has proven its descent from 779 A.D., but they even have good claims all the way back to 365 A.D."

"That's about the oldest family tree I've heard of," I said, "even counting my wife's, which goes back to the 800's. You yourself were you born here?"

"No, I was born in England, but I spent most of my childhood here, always loved the place, the boats, the people. Five years ago I inherited the place from my mother. When I'm not here, I live outside of Chicago."

I asked the Major what his mother's family name was and it turned out to be O'Malley—the famous O'Malley clan of which Grania O'Malley, the pirate queen of the 16th century, was not its greatest but certainly its best-known member. Then a sudden impulse struck me. During lunch, which we had had in the big downstairs room to the right of the entrance door, Sybil had slipped me a piece of paper, murmuring that it was something that had "come" to her. The name rang a bell and I pulled it out of my pocket now.

Scribbled on it were the words "Timothy . . . Mother . . . O'Malley." There was, of course, a mother O'Malley—the Major's own!

"During the times you've been here, Major," I continued now, "have you ever noticed anything unusual?"

The Major nodded. "About six years ago, the following happened. I was asleep in my room upstairs, when suddenly I woke up; at the end of my bed I saw standing an old maidservant; Annie O'Flynn was her name—she had been a maid of my grandmother's.

"I was completely lucid now, having gone to bed at a normal time the night before. My talking to this ghost woke my wife up, and I pointed her out to my wife, saying—'Look, Annie O'Flynn is here, and she's got a friend with her,' for there was another woman with the maid. When I said this, the ghostly maid smiled at me, apparently happy at being recognized. My wife did not see them, but she can attest to the fact that I was fully awake at the time."

"Amazing," I conceded. "What did you do about it?"

"Well, the next morning I went down to talk to Tommy Moran, an old man who works for us and knows a great deal about the people here, and after I described the other ghost to him he was able to identify her as a local friend of Annie's who had passed on also."

"Was that the first time in your life that you've had a psychic experience?"

"Oh no; for instance when I was in the South of France, where I was brought up, I was going up to see some friends who lived just above Nice, and I was with a friend. We had sat down for a moment on a bridge leading into this chateau when we heard the sound of horses and a coach going at full speed. I said to my friend, let's get out of the way because someone's coach has run away! But the noise just went past us and continued on, no coach, no horses! So we continued to our friend Col. Zane's house. When we told him of our experience he laughed. 'That's nothing, really,' he explained. 'That goes on all the time there. It's a ghost coach.' "

"Any other incidents?" I asked with expectation. Obviously, Major Blackwell was gifted with the sixth sense.

"The only other one was here when I dug up the tomb of

Dermot MacGrania." Grania is Irish for grace, incidentally, and it is pronounced more like "gronia."

"I've seen the monolith outside the house, down towards the back end of the estate," I said. "What's the story of that tomb?"

"I started to dig, because I am terribly interested in archaeology. One night I dreamt that I was working on it, as usual, when the stone moved and out from under the stone came this extraordinary figure who was dressed in a kilt and leggings around his feet, and he advanced towards me and I was never so frightened in my life. I couldn't get to sleep at all, and the next morning I went down to the pier, because the two men who had been working on the diggings with me lived across the water and came over by boat.

"Before they landed, they told me immediately, 'We're very, very sorry, but we will not do any more work on the tomb of Dermot MacGrania!'

"Evidently, they too had been frightened off. I have not touched it since then, and that was thirty years ago. I won't permit any digging at the tomb, unless it is for the *good* of it—for I feel that at the time I was not looking into it for that reason, but rather in the hope of finding treasure, and that is why I was stopped."

"This tomb is a pre-Christian relic, is it not?" I asked after a moment of pensive contemplation. Suddenly the 20th century was gone and the very dawn of history was upon us.

"Similar graves exist up in County Sligo. According to the legend told about this particular grave, when Dermot escaped with Grania, they were caught here and killed and buried here by his enemies. That was about 1500 B.C. This is, of course, the very beginning of Irish history."

"Has anyone else had any unusual experience at this tomb?"

"None that I know of. But there have been psychic experiences in the house itself."

I settled back in the comfortable leather chair in the Major's study and listened as Major Blackwell calmly unfolded the record of ghosts at beautiful Ross House.

"Miss Linda Carvel, a cousin of mine, has seen the old maid walking up and down and my wife and I have heard someone walking up and down where the original stairs used to be."

The Major showed me the spot where the wall now covered the stair landing. Only the main staircase exists today.

The former staircase was at the front of the house but structural changes had made it unnecessary.

"My wife has heard it at least four or five times a week. She has also heard the door knocked on."

"Almost like a maidservant," I observed.

"Did anyone *see* the maid?"

"Yes, Linda Carvel actually saw her walking into that front room. This was only two years ago. Everybody had gone to church, and there was nobody in the house at the time except my wife, myself, my daughter and Linda. Linda suddenly came into the room to us, white as a sheet. 'I just saw a woman walk into Granny's room,' she said. 'She was dressed in a white and blue uniform—a starched uniform.' I discussed this with Tommy Moran and he confirmed that that was the uniform the maids wore in my grandmother's time!"

"What do you make of it, Major?"

"I think it is the same one, Annie, who came to see me. She died a normal death, but she was fantastically attached to the family and the house. She spent her whole life here. She married a man named John O'Flynn, a tailor, but she adored it here and even after she left she came back all the time bringing us gifts."

"Have any other phenomena been observed here?"

"In the drawing room, downstairs, Tommy Moran and all his sons have seen two people sitting in front of the fireplace. I know nothing about them firsthand, however. My cousin, Peter O'Malley, also has seen them. He is the one also who had a shocking experience. He saw the most terrible face appear in the window of the drawing room."

"What exactly did he see?" I was all ears now. The whole atmosphere seemed loaded with electricity.

"I wasn't here at the time, but he just says it was a most terrible face. That was ten years ago."

"What about Inishdaff Island, Major?" I asked.

"There is an old monastery there I hope to restore. We've got the records back to 1400 and there it says 'church in ruins.' The peninsula we are on now, where the house stands, also turns into an island at high tide, incidentally, and the path of the pilgrims going over to that ruined church can still be traced. The road would not have been built for any other reason."

"You didn't see anything unusual on the island, though?"

"No, I didn't, but Tommy Moran, and some other relative of mine—actually four people altogether—did. The island has always been considered . . . that there is *something wrong with it*."

We got to talking about the other members of the family now; Mrs. Blackwell had been unable to join us at lunch since she was staying at Castlebar with their fourteen-year-old daughter, who was in the hospital there because of a broken leg. It appeared, however, that there was more to that accident than a casual mishap.

"The extraordinary thing about it is this. The night before it happened, she dreamt that an ambulance drove up to the *front* of the house. Now the front of the house is blocked off to cars, as you saw. So every car must come through the *back*. She saw the ambulance come to the front entrance, however, pick *someone* up and drive off. Also, the ambulance did not have a red cross or other familiar sign on it, but a circular thing in Irish writing! That was exactly the ambulance that came up the next evening and picked *her* up; it was a Volkswagen ambulance with an Irish inscription on the side in a circle just as she had described it to us! Edie is definitely psychic also."

"So it seems," I said. "Anything else about her I might want to know?"

"One time she dreamt she saw Grandmother—my mother—and described her perfectly in every detail. Being terrified of ghosts, Edie, in her dream, pleaded with my mother's apparition not ever to have to see a ghost again. Granny promised her she wouldn't, but she would always *know*."

There were two more points of psychic interest, I discovered. The unexplained putting on of lights and opening of doors in the nursery, and something else that I only learned towards the end of our most enjoyable stay. But in a way it made a perfect finale.

Right now everybody was handed heavy clothing and over-shoes, for we would be sailing—well, motorboating—to the island across the bay and it was wet and chilly, the Major assured us. Cathy looked like a real outdoor girl in the Major's fur jacket, and Sybil was so heavily bundled up she scarcely made the entrance to the cabin of the little boat. The assorted cousins of both sexes also came along in a second boat, and within minutes we were out in the open bay crossing over to the island of Inishdaff, all of which belonged to the Major's estate.

We landed on the island ten minutes later. The sandy beach was most inviting to a swim and Major Blackwell admitted he was working on just such a project. What with the absence of sharks, I felt this to be about the most ideal place to swim in any ocean.

We next scaled the heights of the hill, taking the center of the island, upon which stood the ruined abbey. It was at once clear to me that we were standing close to the roof of that church and that the lower part had simply filled in with soil over the centuries. In one corner of the "elevated floor" was the simple grave of one of Tommy Moran's sons, a Celtic cross watching over him. Otherwise the island was empty.

While the others stood around the ruined abbey, Major Blackwell, Tommy and I mounted the other side of the wall and then descended onto the wet ground. We then proceeded to the top of the island whence we had a magnificent view of all the other islands around us, all the way out to the farthest, which indeed was Ireland's outpost to the sea, beyond which lay America. It was among these many islands and inlets that the pirates of old hid, safe from prosecution by the law.

We fetched some heavy stones from the enclosure of the church and sat down so that Tommy Moran could talk to me about his experiences.

I first questioned him about the frightening face seen here and in the house.

"Mike Sheils told it to me, sir," Tommy Moran began with a heavy brogue. "He worked the glass house with me for years. He was a man not easily frightened. At the time there were blackthorn trees in the burial ground. He was passing through when he heard some noise. He looked over his shoulder and what he saw was a sheep's head with a human body."

"No," I said.

"Yes, sir," Tommy nodded, "it was a head covered with wool the same as sheep. There were three boys in front of Mike. He knocked them down and ran."

"Did you yourself ever have any such experiences here, Tommy?" I reflected that a disheveled human face might very well look like a sheep's head to a simple, imaginative islander used to lots of sheep.

"During me own time, sir," he began, "they were bringing torf to Ross House by boat, that was Mrs. O'Malley's husband, who was gettin' the torf, and they were rowing, two of them, but they had no sail. They wanted to keep as close to the shore as they could. They were brother and sister, Pat Stanton and his sister Bridget. Suddenly a man came down from the burial ground trying to grasp his oar and take it out of the water. Pat rowed like mad to get away; he recalls the man was stark naked, had no clothes on at all. Finally, they got away."

"There was no one living here at the time?"

"No one, no," Tommy assured me, and the Major nodded assent.

I was fascinated by the old man's tales. Surely, Tommy could not have made them up, for what he had said did make some sense when matched with the horrible face looking into the dining room window. Somewhere along the line a human being living like an animal must have found shelter on the desolate island, and, perhaps brought up by animals, this man was taken for a monster. I did not feel that this was a ghost in the sense I use the term.

Tommy told us other tales, some bordering just barely on the supernormal, and then we rejoined the others and went back to the house. It was time for me to question Sybil Leek about her impressions of the church and burial ground.

"There were impressions, but not a presence as we understand it, Hans," Sybil explained, "but I strongly urge that the place be excavated, for there might be some works of art underneath. There is also a passage, which we discovered this afternoon, on the right hand side. The high altar connecting with the first monastic cell."

We had returned now to the house, and took off the heavy clothing the Major had lent us for the journey. While tea was being prepared, we grouped ourselves around the fireplace, waiting.

It was then that I recalled a chance remark Sybil had made to me earlier about a man she had met when we first came to the house, prior to lunch. Perhaps we could sort this out now, before Tommy Moran left for his chores.

"I left the main party in the house for a while, because I wanted to be on my own," Sybil explained, "so I walked through the path leading to the wrought iron gate which led into a garden. I walked right down as far as I could go, until I came to an open space which was on the other side of the garden to where I had started. I reached the tomb. I stayed by the tomb for a little while, then I went toward the gate, ready to climb over the gate, and I was in deep thought. So I wasn't surprised to see a man there. To me he looked rather small, but of course I was on higher ground than he was. He wore no hat, but he had peculiar hair, gray hair."

"What did he do when he saw you?"

"He smiled at me, and appeared to come towards me. I was continuing to walk towards him. He said, 'So you have come back again?' and I replied, 'But I haven't been here. I don't know this place.' He turned and walked towards the sea and I turned away and went back."

"Did he look like a ghost to you?"

"You know I never know what a ghost looks like. To me, everything seems the same. I have this difficulty of distinguishing between flesh-and-blood and ghosts."

When I informed Major Blackwell of Sybil's encounter, he was taken aback and said: "My God, she's seen the other one—she's seen the Sea Captain!"

It turned out that there was another ghost he had not told us about when we talked about the house. Sybil, he felt, had not made contact with the ghostly maidservant—perhaps she had found a more permanent niche by now—but somehow had picked up the scent of the ghostly seaman.

I questioned Tommy Moran, who at 75 knew the place better than any other person, what this sea captain business was all about.

"I don't know his name, sir," Tommy said, "but he was in the house about a hundred years ago. He bought this place and he thought so much about it, he went out to England to bring back his wife and family. He said when he was gone that he would come back, dead or alive!

"He died at sea, and he has since been seen by many, always in daylight, always smoking a cigar; Mike Sheils saw him sittin' in the drawing room once. Several people saw him on the stairway and he always just disappeared. One of my sons saw him and it frightened him. He had no hat, but always this cigar. Very black hair, as tall as you are, sir, according to Mike Sheils."

There you have it, a sea captain *without his cap* but with a cigar! On recollection, Sybil was not sure whether she heard him say, "So you've come back again" or "See, I've come back again."

The Haunted Seminary

I FIRST HEARD OF THE HAUNTED ROOM AT MAYNOOTH COLLEGE from Patrick Byrne, who also assured me it would be difficult, if not impossible, to get permission to investigate it. But a Ghost Hunter never says die, so, without further attempting to set up a visit, I decided to read what there was about the seminary itself, and then set out for it.

"Founded through the exertions of the Irish Hierarchy by an Act of the Irish Parliament in 1795, Maynooth College became within a century one of the largest ecclesiastical seminaries in the world. From its small beginnings with forty students and ten professors accommodated in a converted dwelling-house, it has grown into a fair academic city of nearly six hundred students and a teaching staff of forty, with noble buildings, spacious recreation grounds and one of the finest churches in Ireland. Between 9,000 and 10,000 priests have been trained here.

"Eamon De Valera, President of Ireland, was formerly attached to the teaching staff.

"Passing between the *Geraldine Castle* (begun by Maurice Fitzgerald in 1176) and the *Protestant church* with its pre-Reformation tower, the avenue skirts *Silken Thomas's Tree* (16th century) and affords a fine view of the original college.

In the center is the two hundred years old *mansion of John Stoyte*, where the first students and professors labored, and behind it the buildings erected for them in 1797-9.

"Spacious cloisters are a feature of the Pugin part of Maynooth, and the cloister beginning at the College Chapel leads through a long array of episcopal portraits and groups of past students to the Library and St. Mary's Oratory.

"The *Junior House* buildings (1832-34) contain the 'Ghost Room' which has been enshrined in a maze of gory legends since its conversion into an oratory (1860). They are flanked by a very pleasant rock garden. Beyond, one glimpses the towering trees of the College Park, stretching to the farm buildings in the distance. Nearby a simple yew glade leads to the *Cemetery*, where so many of the great Maynooth figures of the past now rest, undisturbed by the throbbing life around them as a new generation of Maynooth students prepares to carry on their work."

My appetite was aroused. The following day we started out by car towards Maynooth, which is a little west of Dublin and easily reached within an hour's driving time. Our driver immediately knew what we were looking for, having been with us before, so when we reached the broad gates of the College, he pulled up at the gatekeeper's lodge and suggested I have a chat with him. Unfortunately, it started to rain and the chat was brief, but the man really did not know any more than second- or third-hand information. We decided to see for ourselves and drove past the ruined tower of the old Fitzgerald castle into the College grounds. Walking around just like ordinary tourists, we eventually made our way past the imposing main buildings into the courtyard where, according to the gatekeeper, the haunted dormitory was situated.

It was about four in the afternoon, and very few students were in evidence, perhaps because it was vacation time. The building called Rhetoric House was easy to spot, and we entered without asking permission from anyone—mainly because there was nobody around to ask. We realized, of course, that women were somewhat of an oddity here, but then this was a College and not a Trappist Monastery, and mothers must have visited here now and then, so I felt we were doing nothing sacrilegious by proceeding up the iron stairs of the rather drab-looking dormitory. When we reached the second story—always I first and Catherine and Sybil trailing me, in case they had to beat a hasty retreat—we finally found a human being at Maynooth. A young priest stood in one of the corridors in conversation with another priest, and when he saw me, he abruptly terminated it and came towards me, his curiosity aroused as to what I was doing here. As he later explained to me, some not so honest people had on occasion walked in and walked out with various items, so naturally he had learned to be careful about strangers. I dispelled his fears, however, by introducing myself properly, but I must have been slipshod in introducing my wife Catherine and Sybil Leek, for the good father thought Sybil was Cathy's mother—not that Cathy was not honored!

When I asked for his own name, he smiled and said with the humor so often found in Irish priests: "My name is that of a character in one of James Joyce's novels."

"Bloom," I said, smilingly.

"Of course not."

"Well then," I said thoughtfully, "it must be Finnegan."

"You get A for that. Finnegan it is."

And it was thus that I became friendly with a charming gentleman of the cloth, Father Thomas A. Finnegan, a teacher at Maynooth.

I cautiously explained about our interest in the occult, but he did not seem to mind. To the contrary. Leading the way up the stairs, he brought us into the so-called haunted room.

The wall where the mysterious window had been was now boarded up and a statue of St. Joseph stood before the window. The rest of the room was quite empty, the floor shining; there was nothing sinister about it, at least not on first acquaintance.

I took some pictures and filmed the area as Sybil "poked around" in the room and adjacent corridor. Father Finnegan smiled. It was obvious he did not exactly believe in ghosts, nor was he afraid of them if they existed. He was genuinely fond of Maynooth and respected my historical interest along with the psychic.

"You've heard of the tradition about this room, of course," he said, "but I'm sorry I can't supply you with any firsthand experiences here."

"Do you know of anyone who has had any uncanny feelings in this room?" I asked.

"Well, now, the room was closed in 1860, as you know," the priest replied, "and the people who slept in it prior to that date would not be around now. Otherwise no one has reported anything recently—the room is rarely used, to begin with."

Sybil seemed to sense something unpleasant at this point and hurried out of the room, down the corridor.

"There are two good sources on this room," Father Finnegan said, as if he had read my thoughts. "There is Denis Meehan's book, *Window on Maynooth*, published in 1949, and a somewhat longer account of the same story also can be found in *Hostage to Fortune* by Joseph O'Connor. I'll send you one or both books, as soon as I can get hold of them."

With that, Father Finnegan led us down the stairs and gave us the grand tour of Maynooth College, along the library corridors, the beautiful and truly impressive church of St. Patrick, the garden, and finally the museum opened only about twenty years ago.

We thanked him and went back to our car. I then told the driver to stop just outside the College gates on a quiet spot in the road. Sybil was still under the sway of what we had just seen and heard and I wanted to get her psychic impressions while they were fresh.

"Where exactly were we?" Sybil asked. Despite the priest's tour she was somewhat vague about the place.

"We're at Maynooth, in County Kildare," I replied, and added, "You've been in a haunted room on the third floor of a certain dormitory."

"It's a strange place, Hans," Sybil said. "The downstairs is typical of any religious place, peaceful—but when we went up-stairs I had a great desire to run. It was not fear, and yet—I felt I had to run. I had a strange feeling of an animal."

"An animal?" I repeated.

"A four-legged animal. I had the feeling an animal had fol-lowed us down to what is now an oratory."

"What did you feel in the room itself?"

"Fear."

"Any part of the room in particular?"

"Yes, I went straight to the statue."

"Where the window used to be?"

"I felt I wanted to run. I had the feeling of an animal presence. No human."

"Anything else?"

"I developed a tremendous headache—which I generally do when I am where there has been a tragedy. It is gone now. But I had it all the time when I was on that floor."

"Did you feel anyone went out that window?"

"Yes, for at that moment I was integrated into whatever had happened there and *I could have gone out the window!* I was surprised that there was a wall there."

"Did you feel that something unresolved was still present?"

"Yes, I did. But to me it was a case of going back in time. It was a fear of something following you, chasing you."

I thought of the account of the haunting, given by one of the students—the only one who got away with his life—who had seen "a black shape" in the room. Shades of the Hounds of the Baskervilles!

Had someone brought a large dog to the room and had the dog died there? We will never know for sure. Animal ghosts exist and to the novice such an image could indeed be so fright-ening as to induce him to jump out a window. Then, too, the College was built on old ground where in the Middle Ages a castle had stood, replete with keep, hunters—and dogs. Had something from that period been incorporated into the later edifice?

When we returned to Dublin, I had the pictures taken developed but nothing unusual showed on them.

The following week, Father Finnegan sent me a copy of *Window on Maynooth* by Denis Meehan, a sometime professor at the College who is now a Benedictine monk in the United States, according to Patrick Byrne.

Here then, under the subtitle of "The Buildings of Junior House," is Father Meehan's account of the ghost room at Maynooth.

"For the curious, however, the most interesting feature of Rhetoric House will certainly be the ghost room. The two upper floors are altogether residential, and the ghost room is, or rather was, Room No. 2 on the top corridor. It is now an oratory of St. Joseph. Legend, of course, is rife concerning the history of this room; but unfortunately everything happened so long ago that one cannot now guarantee anything like accuracy. The incident, whatever it may have been, is at least dated to some extent by a Trustee's resolution of October 23rd, 1860. 'That the President be authorised to convert room No. 2 on the top corridor of Rhetoric House into an Oratory of St. Joseph, and to fit up an oratory of St. Aloysius in the prayer hall of the Junior Students.'

"The story, as it is commonly now detailed, for the edification of susceptible Freshmen, begins with a suicide. The student resident in this room killed himself one night. According to some he used a razor; but tellers are not too careful about such details. The next inhabitant, it is alleged, felt irresistibly impelled to follow suit, and again, according to some, he did. A third, or it may have been the second, to avoid a similar impulse, and when actually about to use his razor, jumped through the window into Rhetoric yard. He broke some bones, but saved his life. Subsequently no student could be induced to use the room; but a priest volunteered to sleep or keep vigil there for one night. In the morning his hair was white, though no one dares to relate what his harrowing experiences can have been. Afterwards the front wall of the room was removed and a small altar of St. Joseph was erected.

"The basic details of the story have doubtless some foundation in fact, and it is safe to assume that something very unpleasant did occur. The suicide (or suicides), in so far as one can deduce from the oral traditions that remain, seems to have taken place in the period 1842-48. A few colorful adjuncts that used to form part of the stock in trade of the story teller are passing out of memory now. Modern students for instance do not point out the footprint burned in the wood, or the bloodmarks on the walls."

Ghosts Among the American Irish

S O MANY PEOPLE HAVE LEFT IRELAND DURING THE PAST TWO centuries that there are more Irish outside the Ould Sod than back home. At least, so it seems. But the Irish and their descendants, even if they mix with other strains, seem to retain some of the characteristics of the original Gael. Among these qualities is the second sight, the gift of the psychic.

In America, the ghosts of the Irish are perhaps not quite so *lively* as they are in the old country, but they are still interesting.

Barbara is a young woman with a good background who saw me on a Boston television program and volunteered her own experiences as a result. The following week, she wrote to me.

"My family home, in Duxbury, Massachusetts, which is near Plymouth and the home of such notables as Myles Standish and John Alden, is one of the oldest houses in town although we do not know just how old it is.

"Last February my brother, Edward, and his wife, Doris, and their family moved into the house. Before this my brother, Carl, and my father were there alone after my mother's death nearly a year ago.

"The first occasion of odd happenings was on March 17, St. Patrick's day. We are a very small part Irish—the name is about all that is left, O'Neil. A friend of mine and I went up to the farm to visit. Shortly after we arrived we heard a noise, which to me sounded like a baby whimpering as it awoke and to my sister-in-law a woman moaning. I spoke to Doris and something about her baby was awake. She said no and let it pass until later when she told us that she had heard the same noise earlier in the morning and had gone upstairs to check on the baby. As she stood beside the crib, the baby sleeping soundly, she heard the noise again. She then called to the barn to see if all the dogs were accounted for—which they were.

"Since this first noticed phenomenon the following things have occurred.

"My sister-in-law is keeping a log—I may have omissions.

"1. The upstairs door opened and closed (the latch type door) and a shadow filled the whole staircase. It was a calm, cloudy day and the possibility of a draft is somewhat unlikely. Witnessed by Doris.

"2. My brother, Carl, heard a voice saying 'Bring it back.' This went on for several minutes but it was clear for the full time.

"3. Footsteps upstairs heard by Doris.

"4. Doris went into the front room to see the overstuffed rocker rocking as though someone was in it. After she entered the chair began to stop as though someone got up.

"5. July 4, Doris went upstairs and saw the outline of a man which just seemed to disappear.

"Before Edward and Doris moved in, Carl and my father were living there alone (all are in the house now). There was no one in the house most of the time since my mother died nearly a year ago. During this time the girl who rents the other house on the farm twice saw the outline of a man over there—once sitting in a chair and another time she woke my brothers about this. She is very jittery about it and as a result does not know about the other things.

"I suppose I could go on a bit about the family history. My grandmother tracing her ancestry back to Myles Standish and John Alden; my grandfather from Nova Scotia of Scotch-Irish ancestry. I don't know who it was, but someone who lived in the house hanged himself in the barn.

"Carl is a sensible, hard working dairyman who graduated from the University of Massachusetts. Edward is a scoffer since he has observed nothing, recently discharged from the Navy as a Lieutenant and is a graduate of Tufts University.

"Doris is a very intelligent levelheaded girl who, before these events, would have called herself a scoffer or disbeliever.

"I graduated from Bridgewater Teachers College and at first tried to say that there was a logical explanation to these things but there have just been too many things.

"My friend is an intelligent, clear thinking person.

"I give you this background on the witnesses, not as a bragger or being vain, but to give you an idea of the type of witnesses. We are not the hysterical, imagining type.

"The house has thirteen rooms (not all original) and the ghost seems to roam around at will."

*   *   *

Elizabeth Nealon Weistrop is a renowned sculptress who lives far away from the mainstream of city life in rural New Hampshire. I talked to her the other day when I had occasion to admire a particularly striking bronze medallion she had created for the Society of Medallists. It was a squirrel such as abound in her New England woods.

Mrs. Weistrop's experiences have given her a sense of living with the uncanny, far from being afraid of it or worried.

"What were the most striking examples of your brush with the uncanny—that is of yourself or your family?" I queried her.

"There are many," Mrs. Weistrop replied, "but I'll try to give you the most evidential incidents. For example, in 1954 when our Debby was six years old, the doctor decided she should be taken out of the first grade and remain at home to recover from nervousness that resulted from a serious infection she had recently recovered from. She missed going to school with her sister Betsy, two years older, but played every day with five-year-old Donna Esdale, a neighbor's little girl.

"Our family, my husband, our two girls and I, were living in a cottage in West Dennis on Cape Cod at the time and located a better place in Yarmouthport—a warmer house with a studio I could use for sculpture. Donna's father owned a truck, so we paid him to move us to the new house.

"Three weeks later (we had seen no one from West Dennis), Betsy, Debby and I were eating breakfast and Debby said, 'What happened to Donna?' I said, 'What do you mean?' Debby said, 'Why was Donna's face all covered with blood?'—then Betsy and I explained to Debby that she had just had a bad dream and that Donna was all right, but Debby insisted with questions. 'Did a truck hit her?'—'Did someone hit her in the face?'—'Why was her face all covered with blood?'—and no matter how Betsy and I explained about dreams, Debby refused to understand and asked the same questions.

"Finally, the school bus came. Betsy went to school and Debby looked after her wistfully, wanting to go to school too.

"During the day Debby played with her new black puppy and I was busy working at sculpture and the breakfast session left my mind.

"About nine o'clock that evening, Donna's father, Ralph, came to the studio and asked how everyone was. I said we were all fine and automatically asked for his family. He said, 'All right, except that last night my wife and I were up all night. Donna had nose bleeds all night and her face was just covered with blood!'

"Debby was asleep but Betsy was standing near me and we turned and stared at each other in wonder.

"While living on Cape Cod in 1956, we rented a house from a Mrs. Ridley in West Hyannisport. The house she rented to us had belonged to her mother, a woman in her eighties who had recently died. Mrs. Ridley lived next door with her husband and a daughter, Rodella. I found them pleasant people, proud of their American Indian ancestry and sadly missing the grandmother fondly referred to as 'Gunny.' They spoke of her so often and of her constant activity making repairs on the home she loved, that I almost felt I knew her. When they told me of their own supernatural experiences, they did not find a skeptic in me, as my own mother whom I had loved dearly had been gifted with E.S.P. My mother had been the only child born with a caul [veil]—in an Irish family of eleven children, and as I grew up I became very familiar with my mother's amazing and correct predictions. My own experiences with the unknown had been limited to a strong feeling of a force or power leading and directing me in my work as a sculptor.

"One sunny fall afternoon, I was alone concentrating on a sculpture I was doing of St. Francis. My husband, Harry, was away for the day and our two girls were in school, when I heard a loud thump from the bedroom which our girls shared. This room had been the large sunny bedroom of 'Gunny' and within easy view of where I was working. I stopped work to investigate, expecting to see that a large piece of furniture had collapsed or been overturned. As I searched the room and looked out of the window, I could discover nothing that could have made such a sound. Still puzzled, I walked into the next room, the kitchen, and noted that our highly nervous dog was sleeping soundly—a dog who was always on her feet barking at the slightest sound. The clock in the kitchen said 2:30 and that would give me one half hour more to concentrate on St. Francis, so I went back to work, still wondering.

"That evening after the girls were asleep I walked outside in back of the house and Mrs. Ridley, who was sitting on her back porch, invited me in to her house to have coffee with her, her daughter and her daughter's fiancé.

"While we chatted around the table, Mrs. Ridley told of sitting by her kitchen window that afternoon and having *seen her mother*, 'Gunny,' *just as clear as day, walk up the path from the woods* to our house and go over and knock on her own bedroom window at our house.

"I asked, 'What time was that?' and Mrs. Ridley answered, 'At 2:30.' "

A Final Word for All Hibernophiles

T O THOSE OF YOU WHO ARE LUCKY ENOUGH TO BE IRISH—EVEN
being ten per cent Irish will do to hold the franchise—I need
scarcely sing of the charm that is the Emerald Isle in spite of its
shortcomings, or perhaps because of them—for it is the price
one pays for that completely captivating naturalness of character that goes with it.

But those who reluctantly speak of Ireland as a place one
might visit, and those who wouldn't think of it, perhaps even
those who've been to a Third Avenue saloon and drawn con-
clusions from *that*—I invite to see for themselves that it is true
what the Irish say about themselves..

I have not met any leprechauns, but then I did not look for
any, either. I went to ghost hunt and ghosts I found. Not more
ghosts than in any other country, perhaps, but more colorful
ones, more possessed of the unique spirit—if you'll pardon the
pun—that is so typically Irish: a certain liveliness that makes
even the dead act like the quick, if given half a chance!

Those of my readers who wish to tell me of their own psychic
experiences are cheerfully invited to do so, in writing, whether
they are Irish or merely Hibernophiles or merely human beings

with an interest in the psychic world. But out of deference to the physical world, do enclose a stamped, self-addressed envelope!

HANS HOLZER

September 1966